COGNITIVE AGING

Cognitive Aging: The role of strategies offers a ground-breaking new strategy perspective to understanding the underpinnings of both age-related changes and invariance in human cognition. The book first describes what is currently known about cognitive aging, reviewing the behavioral and neuroimaging data showing how our cognitive performance changes with age during adulthood. Current mainstream models propose that as we age we use the same mental processes as when we are young, only less efficiently. In fact, there is good evidence that as we age, we qualitatively change the ways in which we think, resulting in changes in the types of strategies we use to accomplish cognitive tasks.

Using data from psychology and neuroscience, strategic variations during cognitive aging are illustrated in many cognitive domains, from attention, memory, and problem solving to decision making, reasoning, and language. By investigating the various changes in strategy choice and repertoire, frequency of use, and efficiency of execution as adults grow older, the author provides a better understanding of age-related changes and individual differences in human cognition. Finally the book illustrates how this strategy perspective can be used to address related issues such as pathological aging, relationships, and personality, as well as the role of physical fitness and emotions in cognitive aging.

This advanced textbook will be invaluable to students and researchers on cognitive aging courses, as well as those in the field of gerontology, and professionals in allied areas such as medicine, nursing, and social work.

Patrick Lemaire is a Professor of Psychology at Aix-Marseille University. He is also a member of the prestigious Institut Universitaire de France and has over 130 publications in cognitive aging and related fields.

COGNITIVE AGING

The role of strategies

Patrick Lemaire

Routledge
Taylor & Francis Group

LONDON AND NEW YORK

First published in French 2015 as *Vieillissement cognitive et adaptations stratégiques* by De Boeck Supérieur

First published in English 2016
by Routledge
2 Park Square, Milton Park, Abingdon, Oxon OX14 4RN

and by Routledge
711 Third Avenue, New York, NY 10017

Routledge is an imprint of the Taylor & Francis Group, an informa business

British Library Cataloguing in Publication Data
A catalogue record for this book is available from the British Library

Library of Congress Cataloging in Publication Data
A catalog record for this book has been requested

ISBN: 978-1-138-12137-9 (hbk)
ISBN: 978-1-138-12138-6 (pbk)
ISBN: 978-1-315-65099-9 (ebk)

Typeset in Bembo
by Swales & Willis Ltd, Exeter, Devon, UK
Printed in Great Britain by Ashford Colour Press Ltd

CONTENTS

ACKNOWLEDGMENTS

In writing this book I enjoyed the support of various individuals and institutions. First, thanks to my appointment as a Senior Member of the Institut Universitaire de France, I was granted a partial exemption from teaching duties and additional research funds. I have also benefited from continuous support for my research on aging from the National Center for Scientific Research (CNRS) and from my university, Aix-Marseille University. This research, some of which is discussed in this book, was also financed in part by the National Research Agency (ANR).

Many friends, colleagues, and collaborators read the manuscript, and their comments contributed greatly to improving the final product. I particularly wish to extend my warmest thanks to Fleur Brun, Lucile Burger, Fabienne Colette, André Didierjean, Séverine Fay, Thomas Hinault, Michel Isingrini, François Maquestiaux, Aline Pélissier, Céline Poletti, Andrea Soubelet, Laurence Taconnat, Cécile Tison, Sandrine Vanneste, and Sandrine Vieillard. My thanks also to Editions De Boeck for their constant editorial support in the preparation of the French original.

1

COGNITIVE AGING: A BRIEF OVERVIEW

Chapter outline

The goals of the psychology of cognitive aging

Overall changes in intellectual abilities with aging

Cognitive aging and task constraints

Individual differences in cognitive aging

Conclusions

Between the ages of 20 and 60, we can lose up to 40% of our cognitive abilities. Twenty years later, we have lost a further 20%. These figures describe normal aging. That is, what we can experience if we are not suffering from neurodegenerative disease or other aging-related mental or physical health problems. Research on cognitive aging has made major progress over the last three decades. Whereas aging was once seen as an inevitable process of homogeneous cognitive decline, today we have a much more nuanced understanding. We now know that cognitive aging involves a mosaic of phenomena, of which the deterioration of certain intellectual abilities is just one facet, while the maintenance—and even the improvement—of certain other abilities is another. The general idea defended in this book is that the best way to improve our understanding of cognitive aging is to take a strategy approach. This consists of studying age-related differences and changes in strategic variations (i.e., the repertoire, distribution, execution, and selection of strategies) and using methods which are suitable for assessing these variations. Most of this book will focus on showing how this strategy perspective enhances our understanding of cognitive aging. First, this chapter presents a brief overview of the main age-related effects on human cognition (for more detailed and exhaustive presentations, see Craik & Salthouse, 2008; Lemaire & Bherer, 2005, and Salthouse,

2010b). We will then go on to see how the strategy perspective can shed light on these phenomena, as well as uncovering others which would otherwise go entirely unrecognized. The next section begins by reviewing the main goals of the psychology of cognitive aging. The section that follows presents the overall trends in how cognitive performance changes with age, before looking at how various factors modulate these trends. The fourth section discusses observed individual differences in cognitive aging, and the fifth and final section concludes this brief overview.

The goals of the psychology of cognitive aging

The overarching goal of research in the psychology of cognitive aging is to understand how our intellectual abilities change with age during adulthood. This change can result from "normal" aging (i.e., in any individual who does not suffer from dementia or any other age-related neurodegenerative pathology) or from "pathological" aging (i.e., in case of disease). Normal cognitive aging will be the focus of this book.

Researchers pursue a number of objectives in parallel in order to attain this general goal. First, they describe in detail how our cognitive performance changes with age in various domains, from the most basic levels of cognition (such as perception and pattern recognition) to its most highly integrated levels (such as reasoning and decision making). The question in this context is whether certain cognitive functions are more affected by aging than others. Among the affected functions, how much does each one decline? Do certain functions deteriorate more and earlier than others? Do the speed and range of decline vary from one function to another? What kind of involution does each function go through over time? For a given function, does performance on one task decrease more than performance on another task, which assesses a different component of that function? Are some preserved? Does change over time in different functions interact with task constraints? In other words, regardless of the domain of cognition that is studied, the task is to describe what changes (i.e., deteriorates or improves) and what remains stable across ages.

It is not always easy to draw clear conclusions on age-related changes of different functions. For a given function in a given domain (e.g., memory), often large performance differences are observed between young and older participants (e.g., in recall tasks assessing episodic memory); sometimes smaller differences are found (e.g., in episodic memory recognition tasks); and sometimes even no differences with age are observed (e.g., in implicit memory tasks). For example, in studies on implicit memory, some researchers have found no differences between young and older participants when probing implicit memory using word-fragment completion tasks, where participants are shown a group of letters and asked to add letters to this group in order to make a word (e.g., Clarys, Isingrini, & Haerty, 2000; Fay, Isingrini, & Clarys, 2005; for similar results with a motor task, see also Chauvel et al., 2012; Fleischman, Wilson, Gabrieli, Bienias, & Bennett, 2004), or an identification task where participants are shown pictures of objects and are asked to name them (e.g., Mitchell, 1989). In contrast, other researchers have found large differences between young and older participants when they have probed implicit memory using a task requiring participants to spell words aloud (e.g., Davis et al. 1990). On one task, trigram completion (i.e., participants are shown the first three letters of a word and have to complete it with the missing letters to form a word), certain studies have reported deleterious effects of age (e.g., Small, Hultsch, & Masson, 1995; Winocur, Moscovitch & Stuss, 1996), while others have reported no effects (e.g., Clarys et al., 2000; Fay et al., 2005; Nicolas, Ehrlich, & Facci, 1996).

The use of a wide range of tasks, techniques, and measures is required to produce convergent results that reveal the patterns underlying the diversity of findings. By studying differences between domains and tasks, as well as within tasks, psychologists aim at establishing the most detailed and precise possible cartography of how cognition changes with age. Their ambition is to uncover the general characteristics that distinguish cognitive functions and processes which change with aging from those that remain stable. One important general feature that characterizes age-related changes in many cognitive function is costs in processing resources. As we shall see in this book, across a wide range of cognitive domains, the more demanding in processing resources, the larger deleterious aging effects. In sum, the first objective of cognitive aging research is to as precisely and with as many details as possible determine what changes and what remains stable with aging in human cognition.

The next question is whether there are individual differences in how cognitive performance changes with aging. In other words, does aging affect everyone in the same way, or are there individuals whose performance does not decline at all with age, or individuals whose decline is less marked than others? Once these individual differences have been determined and documented with great details, the next task for psychologists is to determine what characterizes individuals who experience greater deficits with aging versus those undergoing much more successful aging. The extent of decline can be assessed both by the number of domains where deficits are observed and by the amount of decline in a given domain. Aging patterns can vary widely. An individual might experience smaller deficits in many domains, or, in contrast, very significant deficits in a smaller number of domains. Moreover, two comparable patterns of cognitive decline (in terms of magnitude and/or number of deficits) can result from different underlying realities (e.g., different cognitive mechanisms are affected). To determine the origins of these individual differences, psychologists study a wide range of variables: Cognitive (e.g., level of formal education), affective (e.g., emotional stability), and personal characteristics (e.g., intro-/extraverted personality, gender, physical health), as well as life history (e.g., profession, stress, trauma) and habits (e.g., diet, exercise, and socio-cultural activities). The study of these variables allows researchers not only to determine what characteristics underlie individual differences, but also to investigate the mechanisms that produce them. It can also yield highly general information on human cognition (e.g., what are the conditions for optimal cognitive plasticity? What conditions are needed to maintain, or even continuously develop, cognitive functioning over the lifespan? What are the limits of our cognitive capacities?).

The third objective of research on cognitive aging is to determine what mechanisms underlie observed changes (as well as stability) in cognitive performance during adulthood. Age, or the passage of time, is in no way the cause of cognitive aging. Instead, what psychologists of cognitive aging try to find out is what happens in our lives as time passes. This chain of events plays out at different levels of the cognitive system, from the molecular and cellular levels all the way up to the most integrated and functional levels of the central nervous system. Psychologists focus more on the functional and behavioral levels, although they increasingly work in close collaboration with researchers in other disciplines which study aging, such as neurosciences and biomedical sciences.

Finally, while the goal of basic research is not to produce immediate solutions to practical problems—given that the usefulness of fundamental discoveries, although very important, is often an unintentional and unpredictable result of the quest for understanding—one of the reasons to value research on aging is that it can lead to applications. There are many such applications, both in pathological aging (improved diagnosis and care for older patients, better support for care-takers) and in normal aging (to help each of us to undergo successful aging). In the case of normal aging, insofar as basic research tells us about the conditions required to age "successfully," its discoveries offer the promise not necessarily of adding more years to life but, as a celebrated phrase puts it, of "adding more life to (years of) life."

Overall changes in intellectual abilities with aging

To study age-related differences in our intellectual abilities, researchers administer various tasks to young adults (between the ages of 20 and 40) and older adults (aged 65 and older). These tasks either assess overall intellectual functions or specifically target certain functions and/or processes. The overall tests include, for example, the famous IQ (intelligence quotient) tests, and offer a general assessment of intellectual abilities and how these abilities change with age. Many studies have used these types of tests and either compared the performance of young and older people (in cross-sectional designs) or else followed the same cohort of participants over many years (longitudinal designs). The results of such studies are illustrated in Figure 1.1. For example, Figure 1.1a shows data from the Seattle Longitudinal Study. These data show the performance of over 1,300 adults tested by Schaie and collaborators (Schaie, 1996) with the Primary Mental Abilities Test assessing reasoning, spatial cognition, perceptual speed, episodic memory, and vocabulary. As can be easily seen, apart from vocabulary, age leads to decreased intellectual performance. Figure 1.1b presents another example, the data from the Berlin Aging Study, in which Baltes and Lindenberger (1997) studied the sensory and intellectual functions of more than 300 participants between the ages of 20 and 103. At the sensory level, they tested visual and auditory acuity. At the intellectual level, they tested information-processing speed, reasoning, memory, knowledge, and verbal fluency. As the data in Figure 1.1b show, aging is accompanied by a steady and continuous decline in all of our sensory and cognitive abilities.

(a)

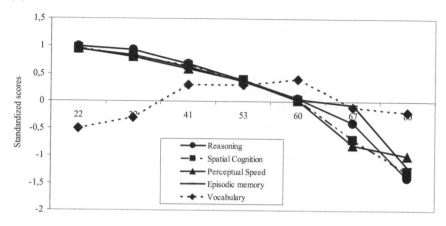

(b)

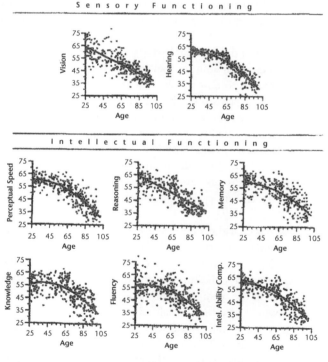

FIGURE 1.1 Changes in intellectual abilities with age: (a) standardized scores on the Primary Mental Abilities Test (following Schaie, 2005); (b) scores on different sensory and cognitive measures from the Berlin Aging Study. (Data from Baltes, P. & Lindenberger, U. (1997). Emergence of a powerful connection between sensory and cognitive functions across the adult lifespan: A new window to the study of cognitive aging. *Psychology and Aging, 12,* 12–21, APA, reprinted with permission.)

Note that similar patterns of change in cognitive performance with age have been observed in longitudinal and cross-sectional studies. The decline with age seems to be (artificially) smaller in longitudinal studies, due to a simple test–retest effect. That is, performing the same tests a number of times, even at intervals of some years, attenuates the decrease in performance with age (Salthouse, 2010a, 2014). As interesting, informative, and valid as these data from psychometric studies on aging are, they are also limited in some ways. The most important of these, regarding what deteriorates and what remains stable with age in human cognition, is that these data suggest that all sensory and intellectual functions (except for vocabulary and knowledge) decline with age, beginning very early and going on steadily and continuously thereafter. And yet, when researchers began to take a cognitive perspective and started to analyze cognition in terms of information-processing operations, they observed that patterns of cognitive change can vary widely according to the domains tested and the tasks used. By breaking down broad intellectual functions into basic processes, researchers arrived at a picture of aging that was much richer and more interesting than the one that had previously been derived from the results of general tests. Here we will look at a few examples of such results from studies on major cognitive functions, such as attention, memory, and problem solving.

In the domain of attention, researchers try to understand how a number of abilities change with age: Our ability to select relevant information for processing and/or to focus on the important aspects of a task (selective attention), to divide our attentional resources between several information sources (divided attention), to flexibly alternate our attentional resources between different tasks or information sources (attentional flexibility), or to remain deeply focused for a prolonged period (sustained attention). A large number of tasks have been used to study the effects of aging on each of these attentional functions (see Maquestiaux, 2013; Pashler, 1998; Johnson & Proctor, 2004, for overviews). Let us look at illustrative examples of these effects from two studies: One on selective attention, the other on sustained attention.

One of the tasks used in the study of selective attention is the detection of a target item among other (distractor) items. For example, Farkas and Hoyer (1980) asked young and older participants to detect a T that was rotated by 90 degrees in three different experimental conditions. In the first condition, the target letter was presented on its own. In the second condition, it was presented along with distractors (other letters) which were not visually similar to it. In the third condition, it was shown among visually similar distractors. In addition to the finding that young people performed better at the task overall, the data also showed that older people had more difficulty ignoring distractors (Figure 1.2a). Unlike young people, older people took more time to detect the letter when it was presented along with other letters (similar or different); performance time increased still more with age in the condition where the distractors were similar to the target. These findings pointed to the idea that older participants were more easily distracted by irrelevant stimuli, which suggests an age-related deficit in inhibitory mechanisms.

In a study on sustained attention, Giambra and Quilter (1988) asked participants aged between 20 and 60 years or over to perform the Mackworth Clock Test. In this task, participants fixate on a pointer which makes a movement every second. From time to time, the pointer makes two movements in a single second, or a single movement over two seconds. The participants' task is to press a button as quickly as possible to indicate when the pointer deviates from its regular pace of movement. As Figure 1.2b shows, detection times and rates of omissions (failures to detect

(a)

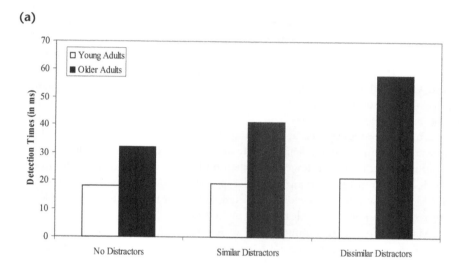

(b)

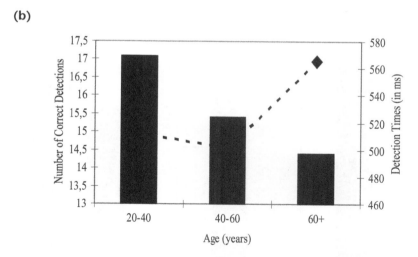

FIGURE 1.2 Age-related differences in attentional abilities. (a) Selective attention (data from Farkas & Hoyer, 1980); (b) sustained attention (Giambra & Quilter, 1988). These data show that our attentional abilities decrease with age.

irregular movements) were higher in older people than in young people. Older people's disadvantage in detection times and rate of omissions became even greater in the second half of the experiment. These results suggest that, with age, we find it increasingly difficult to continue focusing on a task for a long time.

In the domain of memory, researchers seek to understand change with age in our abilities to encode information, retain it, and recall it when needed. This information can be declarative (knowing *that*) or procedural (knowing *how*).

In one of the first studies on age-related differences in declarative memory, Smith (1977) read a list of 20 words a single time to young adults (20–40 years), middle-aged adults (40–60 years) and older adults (more than 60 years) and tested their memory using either a free-recall task or a cued-recall task. The number of words correctly recalled in both of these tasks steadily decreased with age (Figure 1.3a). In a study on aging and procedural memory, Charness and Campbell (1988) trained participants to mentally calculate the square of a two-digit number (e.g., $12 \times 12 = 144$; $27 \times 27 = 729$) using an algorithm comprising several steps. As Figure 1.3b shows, all three groups of participants became increasingly quick at executing this algorithm with practice. However, both maximum speed and learning rate decreased with age. Young adults attained their maximum speed in fewer trials than middle-aged participants, who in turn made quicker progress than the older participants. Moreover, this maximum speed decreased as the age of the participants increased. Aging thus leads to a decrease in our abilities to learn new procedures.

Many studies on reasoning have also shown that performance decreases with age. For example, Arenberg (1982) administered the poisoned-foods task to

(a)

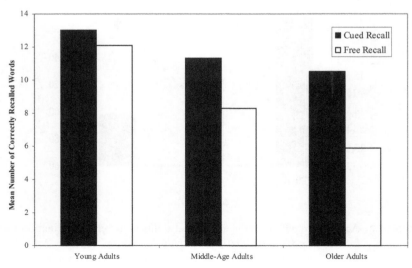

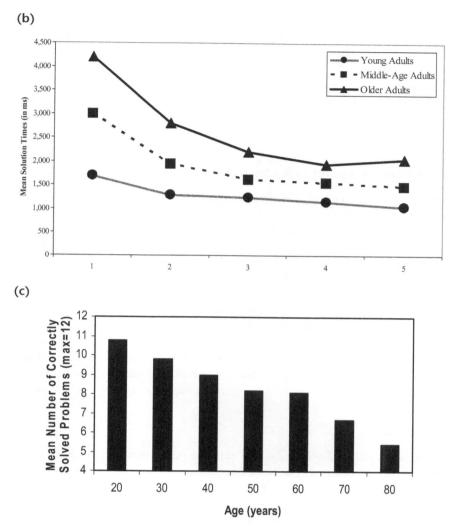

FIGURE 1.3 Age-related differences in memory and reasoning. (a) Declarative memory (data from Smith, 1977); (b) procedural memory (data from Charness & Campbell, 1988); and (c) inductive reasoning (data from Arenberg, 1982).

participants from age 20 to 80 and above. In this task, participants are given instructions such as these:

> A meal consists of four dishes (A, B, C, D). For example, an appetizer, a meat dish, a vegetable dish, and a dessert. For each dish, there is a choice of two foods (1 or 2). For example, the appetizer can be either a salad or cold cuts, the dessert either ice cream or a fruit. Certain meals are poisoned. This can

be determined by the type of food chosen for each dish. Find the poisoned food by creating menus: In each case you will be told whether or not your menu is poisoned.

The number of inductive reasoning problems correctly solved (out of 12), appearing in Figure 1.3c, showed a substantial, steady, and continuous decrease in performance with increasing age, from nearly 11 problems solved at age 20 to around five at age 80.

Cognitive aging and task constraints

Cognitive functions do not change homogeneously with aging, as the results presented above might seem to suggest. That is, performance does not decrease to the same extent or at the same speed in all domains and all tasks. In reality, the way in which different forms of cognitive performance change over time is influenced by the different constraints that apply to each task/domain. Thus, performance decreases, increases, or remains stable with age depending on the type of stimulus used, the situation that participants are tested in, and the type of constraints that the task requires them to take into account. In all domains of cognition, these constraints influence participants' performance as well as magnitudes of age-related differences in performance. The extent of this influence varies depending on the domain and the task. Let us look at a few examples that illustrate how age-related decreases in performance vary with the type of task, instructions, and stimuli that are used. The examples are drawn from studies on perception, memory, reasoning, and language.

Perception

Hommel, Li, and Li (2004) gave young and older participants a target detection task in different experimental conditions. The participants were shown shapes (circles, squares) on a computer screen. They had to say whether each set of shapes contained a filled circle (half did, the other half did not). The sets included two, eight, or 14 distractors. The distractors could be circles (i.e., the same shape as the target) in so-called homogeneous sets, as well as squares (i.e., some of the distractors differed in shape from the target) in so-called heterogeneous sets. Figure 1.4 shows data from the conditions with seven and 13 distractors. As can be seen, in addition to the effect of age on correct target detection times (with older participants showing longer detection times), the differences between young and older participants were greater for heterogeneous sets with more distractors.

Memory

Numerous studies on memory have found that the differences between young and older participants vary as a function of whether they are performing an incidental-recall task (where they are not informed in advance that they will

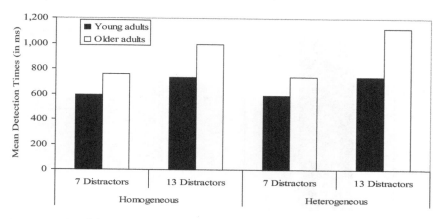

FIGURE 1.4 Modulations of age-related differences in selective attention (data from Hommel et al., 2004).

have to recall the material to be learned) or an intentional-recall task (where they know that they will have to perform a recall task after the encoding phase). For example, Light and Zelinski (1983) asked young and older subjects to memorize objects and their locations on a map. The participants were tested either in an intentional-learning condition (i.e., they were asked to learn the items and their locations in order to recall both later), or in an incidental-learning condition (i.e., they were instructed to memorize the objects, but were not told that their memory of the objects' locations would also be tested). During the recall phase, the participants had to recognize the 12 objects they had seen out of a set of 18, and to indicate their locations on an unmarked map. The older participants did substantially less well on the task, particularly in the incidental-learning condition (Figure 1.5). In another example, Taconnat, Clarys, Vanneste, Bouazzaoui, and Isingrini (2007) tested young and older adults after showing them 24 pairs of six- to nine-letter words (e.g., *house–soldier*) on a computer screen for 5 seconds each. The participants were asked to indicate how closely associated the two words were, using a Likert scale from 1 to 5 (1: weakly associated; 5: strongly associated). They then performed a cued-recall test (i.e., they had to recall the second word in each pair) in two conditions. In the high-support condition, the participants' cue was the first word in each pair and the first three letters of the second word (e.g., *house, sol____*). In the low-support condition, their only cue was the first three letters in the second word from the pair (e.g., *sol____*). As Figure 1.6 shows, both age groups performed better in the high-support condition than in the low-support condition, but the difference was larger in the older group.

A final example is the study of Park and Shaw (1992), who found that the implicit memory performance of young and older adults differed little, or even not at all, whereas older adults performed worse than young adults on an explicit

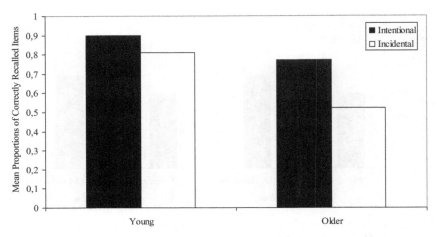

FIGURE 1.5 Modulations of age-related differences in memory performance (data from Light & Zelinski, 1983).

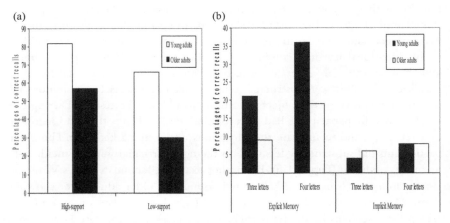

FIGURE 1.6 (a, b) Modulations of age-related differences in memory performance ((a) data from Taconnat et al., 2007 and (b) from Park & Shaw, 1992).

memory task (their data are summarized in Figure 1.6b). In both tasks, participants first learned a set of words and then were shown three- or four-letter word stems. Their task was to complete the words either with the words they had previously learned (explicit memory) or with any word that came to mind (implicit memory). As the data show, young and older participants showed comparable percentages of correct recall on the implicit memory task, whereas the older group performed worse on the explicit memory task.

Reasoning

The data presented in Figure 1.7 show that decreases in inductive reasoning performance with age interact with the type of information that participants are asked to process. In this study, Salthouse and Prill (1987) gave number series problems to young and older participants. In easy problems, the participants were shown a series of numbers, such as 19-22-25-28-31, and asked to indicate what number comes next in the series. They were also presented with moderately difficult problems, with series such as 63-91-65-94-67, and difficult problems, with series such as 84-66-52-42-36. The data clearly showed that the more difficult the required inductive inference, the larger the increase in solution times for these inductive reasoning problems. In a study on deductive reasoning, Salthouse (1992) gave participants between the ages of 25 and 75 three categories of reasoning problems. The first category involved a single premise (e.g., "C and D do the same. If C increases, will D decrease?"), the second two premises (e.g., "H and I do the same. G and H do the opposite. If G increases, will I decrease?"), and the third three premises (e.g., "W and X do the opposite. V and W do the same. X and Y do the opposite. If V increases, will Y decrease?"). As the data summarized in Figure 1.8 (right panel) show, performance decreased with age only for problems with two or three premises, whereas for problems with a single premise it remained stable. It also decreased more for problems with three premises than for those with two premises. In other words, the more information is required (i.e., number of premises), the larger the negative effects of age on deductive reasoning. Inferential mechanisms are thus not destroyed with age, but using them becomes more difficult when participants must integrate a larger amount of information.

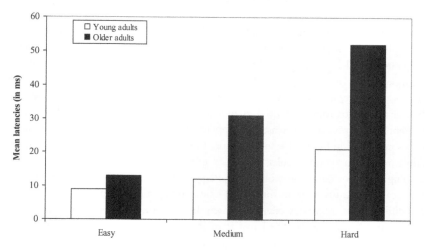

FIGURE 1.7 Modulations of age-related differences in inductive reasoning (data from Salthouse & Prill, 1987).

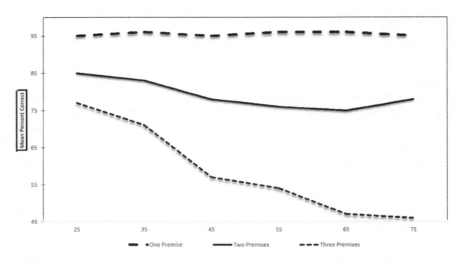

FIGURE 1.8 Modulation of age-related differences in inductive reasoning (data from Salthouse, 1992).

Language

Regarding language, psychologists seek to understand how the processes involved in our abilities to produce and understand language change with age. Research focuses on the various linguistic processing units (words, sentences, texts) and on both spoken and written language. At the word level, psychologists seek to discover how age affects processes like phonological and orthographic processing, which are crucial in accessing the lexicon. As in the other domains of cognition, psychologists study the effects of known variables in order to vary the difficulty of these processes, and examine the resulting effects on performance differences between young and older participants. For example, Allen, Bucur, Grabbe, Work, and Madden (2011) gave young and older participants a word-reading task in different experimental conditions. Certain words were phonologically regular (e.g., *beam*), meaning they are pronounced as they are written; others were irregular (e.g., *have*); some were frequent, others more rare. Additionally, half of the words were presented in all lowercase letters, whereas the other half were presented in a mix of lowercase and uppercase letters. As the irregular word-naming times presented in Figure 1.9 show, besides the longer reading times observed in older adults relative to young adults, frequency effects (i.e., reading times for rare words–reading times for common words) were larger when all the letters were presented in lowercase (+132 ms) than in the mixed-case condition (+102 ms). More interestingly, the difference in frequency effects between the two conditions was larger in the older participants (+150 ms vs. +113 ms) than in the younger participants (+114 ms vs. +90 ms). This Age × Condition × Frequency interaction is important because, as the authors point out, it suggests that the mixed-case condition disturbed lexical processing in older adults during the reading task. Mixed-case presentation apparently prevented

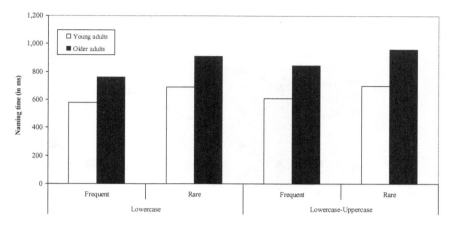

FIGURE 1.9 Modulation of age-related differences in language (data from Allen et al., 2011).

older adults from focusing as much as they do normally on larger grapho-phonemic units, which slowed their performance, more so for frequent words.

Individual differences in cognitive aging

Along with intra-individual differences (i.e., differential aging in different cognitive domains, tasks, and experimental conditions), inter-individual differences are also found (i.e., different individuals aging differently). Beyond simply observing that certain individuals experience earlier and/or larger declines, either in general or in particular domains, researchers seek to understand these differences. They aim at determining what individual characteristics are associated to these inter-individual differences. Understanding the mechanisms underlying these differences may not only allow us to explain them, but also to offer potential ways to counter or slow age-related cognitive declines. Such inter-individual differences have been observed both in large-scale studies on how cognitive performance changes with age (using batteries of psychometric tests) and in laboratory studies focused on specific cognitive functions and processes.

For example, as Figure 1.10a illustrates, the Seattle Longitudinal Study (Schaie, 2005; see also Salthouse, 2009a, b, 2010a) showed that one or two cognitive abilities began to decline in certain individuals beginning in their 30s (not necessarily the same abilities in each person). It also showed that:

- as of age 65, everyone has at least one declining cognitive ability;
- as of age 80, two abilities have declined in at least 80% of individuals;
- at age 90, three abilities have deteriorated in around 50% of the population;
- even at age 90, no one has experienced deterioration in all five abilities.

(a)

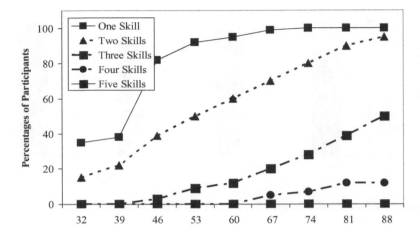

(b)

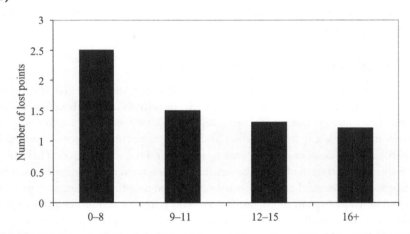

FIGURE 1.10 Inter-individual differences in cognitive aging assessed by psychometric tests or tests of general cognitive efficiency. (a) Percentages of individuals with one to five declining mental abilities, by age (data from Schaie, 1996); (b) decrease in Mini–Mental State Examination score over 11.5 years by level of education (data from Lyketsos et al., 1999).

In other words, these data show that, in some individuals, advancing age leads to the decline of one, two, or more abilities, and that the number of abilities that decline with age differs between individuals.

Besides studying individual differences in age-related declines in performance on tasks which rely on a well-understood set of processes, cognitively oriented research has also succeeded in identifying a set of individual characteristics which modulate cognitive aging. Data from numerous studies suggest that cognitive decline varies with levels of education, profession, lifestyle, and socio-cultural activities, physical condition.

For example, Figure 1.10b is based on data published by Lyketsos, Chen, and Anthony (1999) showing decreases in scores (out of 30) on the Mini-Mental State Examination (MMSE), a test of overall cognitive function, over 11.5 years in a large sample of participants, according to their number of years of education. Although the MMSE is a very general and relatively insensitive test, it can clearly be seen that general cognitive efficiency decreased considerably more in participants with a lower level of education.

Note that general intelligence tests are not the only ones to have revealed inter-individual differences in aging. Such differences have also been found with tests of specific cognitive functions and processes, such as attention and memory. For example, the data of Bruyer, Van der Linden, Rectem, and Galvez (1995), shown in Figure 1.11a, showed that, in a Stroop task, age differences in performance in the interference condition decreased with increasing levels of education, suggesting that attentional processes (and in particular inhibition) decrease less with aging in more educated participants. Another example is the study of Mathy and Van der Linden (1995), who found that, in a story recall task, the number of correctly recalled statements decreased with age only in participants with a relatively low level of education (Figure 1.11b).

Other factors have also been shown to modulate the effects of aging, such as level of expertise, socio-cultural activities, lifestyle, physical condition, and cognitive training. For example, expertise in a domain can modulate age-related cognitive decline. The data from Salthouse (1984) presented in Figure 1.11c illustrate how, in that study, typing expertise neutralized the effects of aging on inter-key interval (time between keystrokes in typing) and on a laboratory tapping task. The lengthening of inter-key and tapping latencies increased with age only in participants with a low level of typing expertise. Another example is the modulatory effects of physical activity on age-related cognitive declines (see Bherer, Erickson, & Liu-Ambrose, 2013, for a review). Physical activity has been shown to moderate the deleterious effects of age on many cognitive functions. As an illustration, Figure 1.11d shows a portion of the data of Boucard et al. (2012), which illustrate the Age × Physical Activity interaction on interference effects on the Simon task. In the version of the Simon task used by Boucard et al., participants were shown either the word RIGHT or the word LEFT, along with an arrow pointing either right or left. In a given block of trials, the participants had to press a response button located on the right side when the word RIGHT (or, in another block of trials, the rightward arrow) appeared, and a response button located on the left when they saw the word LEFT (or the leftward arrow). In half of the items, the word and the arrow were congruent (i.e., the response corresponding to both stimuli was the same, as when the word RIGHT appeared along with an arrow pointing to the right). In the other half of the items, the word and the arrow were incongruent (i.e., the response corresponding to the two stimuli was different, as when the word RIGHT appeared along with an arrow pointing to the left). The difference between the congruent and incongruent conditions, called the interference effect, results from the need to use inhibition in the incongruent condition. Participants have to inhibit the irrelevant response in order to respond to the relevant cue. The young and older participants tested by Boucard et al. were either sedentary or active (i.e., they regularly engaged in one or more physical activities). As Figure 1.11d shows, the interference effects were larger in sedentary participants than in active participants, and the difference between active and sedentary individuals was larger in older than in young participants. Given that, in principle, the smaller the interference effects, the more efficient the inhibition, these results suggest that inhibitory

(a)

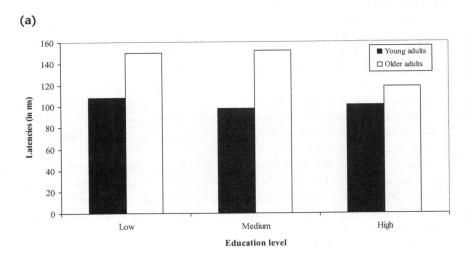

(b)

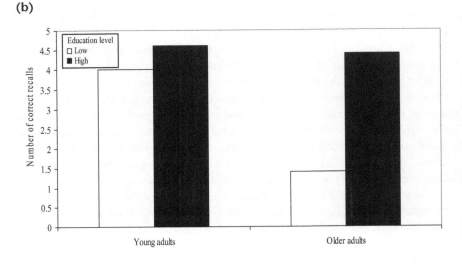

(c)

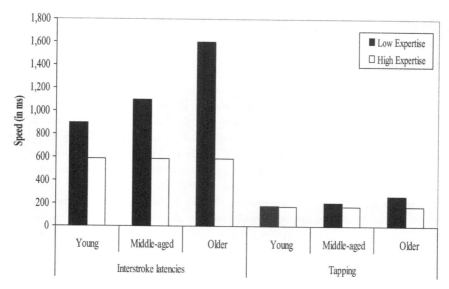

(d)

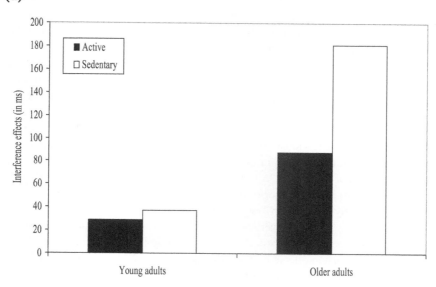

FIGURE 1.11 Modulations of the effects of aging by education in different cognitive domains: (a) inhibition in the Stroop task (Bruyer et al., 1995); (b) episodic memory (Mathy & Van der Linden, 1995); (c) typing speed (Salthouse, 1984); (d) inhibition in the Simon task (Boucard et al., 2012).

mechanisms are more efficient in active older participants than in those who are sedentary. In sum, aging has a lesser negative effect on inhibitory abilities in older adults who regularly practice one or more physical activities.

Conclusions

Research on cognitive aging has made substantial progress over the last three or four decades. It has led to significant advances in our knowledge about how our cognitive performance and abilities change with aging. Although research in the area is flourishing and there is every reason to expect and hope for many more new discoveries, a number of relatively general conclusions can be drawn from currently available results. It is already possible to present a fairly clear and precise summary of the major changes in cognition that occur with aging.

First of all, most of our intellectual abilities decline with age. Some decrease more than others (e.g., attention and memory decline more than reasoning and decision making). Certain abilities begin to decrease very early (e.g., switching starts to decrease at age 16); others do not begin to decrease until we are in our 50s or 60s (e.g., deductive reasoning); still others begin to decrease only when we are in our 80s or 90s (such as language), or may even never decline at all (in certain individuals). When aging does lead to decreased performance in a cognitive domain, then the more complex the task, the greater the decrease (this is what psychologists call the Age × Complexity interaction, which is observed in all cognitive domains). For example, older adults have more difficulty than young adults with memorizing a list of abstract words compared to a list of concrete words, even if the two lists contain the same number of words. Another example is that age has a lesser effect on reasoning from two premises than on reasoning from three or more premises. In all domains of cognition, most of the mental operations used to perform a task are slowed—by up to 70% in certain individuals and/or for certain intellectual activities.

Moreover, there are very large individual differences in the effects of aging. On the one hand, intra-individual differences mean that a given person can experience pronounced cognitive decline in one or more domains while showing stable performance in other domains. On the other hand, the existence of inter-individual differences means that, all other things being equal, some people experience very large and/or early decline (in one or more cognitive domains), whereas others remain cognitively alert until very late in life. The underlying reasons for these differences are still poorly understood, but they include factors relating to quality of life, personal history, and level of education, as well as biological (such as heredity and the physiological efficiency of brain functions) and health factors. In short, individuals who received longer formal education, who live a relatively healthy life (nutrition, sleep, exercise), who engage in socio-cultural activities, and who do intellectually stimulating work tend to experience less age-related cognitive decline (or even preserved cognitive function).

Recent work suggests that individuals who age well have significant cognitive reserves, potentiated notably by factors such as prolonged schooling, a challenging occupation, and stimulating leisure activities. People who age "successfully" also tend to use many compensatory mechanisms to deal with the effects of aging. These mechanisms can be at the cognitive level (e.g., use of mental strategies which are easier to implement) and/or at the physiological level (e.g., activation of additional brain areas which other older people do not use when performing a cognitive task).

Above and beyond the primary goals of mapping out changes in cognitive performance with aging and characterizing inter-individual differences in those changes, it is important to understand the mechanisms responsible for age-related cognitive changes. Several approaches can be taken to pursue this objective, as we will see in the rest of this book. One of the approaches that the book particularly focuses on is the strategy approach (or perspective). It consists in examining changes in cognitive performance over time from the perspective of the strategies that participants use to perform different tasks. This approach follows in the tradition of cognitive psychology, which analyzes cognition in terms of information-processing operations (or in terms of mechanisms). This perspective has been extremely fruitful in the psychology of aging. Its fundamental aspects (the definition of "strategy," distinctions between strategies, methods for studying them, relevant strategic dimensions) are discussed in the next chapter.

2

COGNITIVE STRATEGIES

Chapter outline

Strategy: Definitions and properties

Theoretical distinctions between strategies

Empirical distinctions between strategies

Strategic variations and aging

Psychologists have two overarching goals: To describe behaviors as precisely and accurately as possible, and to explain them. To achieve these two fundamental goals, they carry out empirical studies (i.e., research based on data). Data can be derived from direct observations (natural observations, clinical cases) and from laboratory experiments and quasi-experiments. These provide measures of behavior. For example, psychologists interested in memory try to describe what conditions are associated to the best memory performance. To do this they perform laboratory experiments on memory where, for example, they may give participants lists of words to learn and then ask them to recall as many words as possible. They then offer one or several explanations for any observed difference in memory performance between experimental conditions. To explain behavior, cognitive psychologists try to discover the sequence of mental processes (or mental operations, or information-processing operations) that are involved (Fodor, 1972). With this aim in mind, studying cognitive strategies is a fruitful way to understand cognition and behavior in general. Insofar as discovering the strategies participants use to successfully perform a cognitive task consists in uncovering the sequence of processes that they use to do so, studying cognitive strategies is thus an ideal way to explain cognitive performance. And indeed, performance differences between conditions (or groups of participants) often result at least in part from the use of different strategies (or sequences of processes). Describing the strategies that participants use in a cognitive task is therefore an extremely fruitful approach to understanding cognitive performance. It is the best approach to establishing a mechanistic explanation of cognitive performance (i.e., an explanation in terms of cognitive mechanisms or processes). This chapter begins with some definitions (e.g., strategy), distinctions (e.g., strategies and heuristics), and considerations on a strategy approach to human cognition. It then looks at how psychologists distinguish a number of strategies both on the theoretical and empirical levels. Finally, it describes a conceptual framework that is useful for studying strategic variations during aging.

Strategy: Definitions and properties

What is it that we call a "strategy"? In one of the founding works of cognitive psychology, Newell and Simon (1972) defined a strategy as a method used to complete a cognitive task. Since then, many definitions have been proposed. They differ on various points (e.g., whether or not strategies must be consciously implemented, whether or not participants must be able to describe them verbally, and whether or not they necessarily improve performance). However, they all have in common that they consider a strategy to be "a procedure or set of procedures for achieving a higher level goal or task" (Lemaire & Reder, 1999, p. 365). Higher-level goals/tasks are simply cognitive tasks. For psychologists, then, the challenge in this context is to determine what sequence of mental operations or procedures (also known as "information-processing steps") a participant uses to complete a cognitive task.

Distinction between strategies, heuristics, procedures, and mechanisms

The various definitions of the concept of strategy allow us to arrive not only at a shared understanding of what a strategy is, but also of what a strategy is not. A strategy in cognitive psychology is not quite the same thing as a military strategy, for example. A military strategy consists in finding a way to win a war. This type of strategy aims to accomplish a single goal: Winning. Succeeding at a task is not the only goal of a cognitive strategy; it is the means by which the participant completes the task. The use of a strategy sometimes leads to success when it is correctly executed and appropriate, and other times to failure (or error). When they seek to explain cognitive performance, psychologists must explain not only how subjects succeeded, but also how they failed. This means that the study of strategies includes understanding not only strategies which lead to success at a task, but also those that lead to failure.

Sometimes psychologists reduce "strategy" to its military meaning and suggest that participants are being strategic when they use strategies which improve their cognitive performance. For example, in studies on memory, some researchers say that participants act strategically (i.e., use strategies) to improve their memory performance. Thus, from this perspective, participants are acting "strategically" when they use a strategy based on forming mental images to encode a list of words, and nonstrategically when they mentally repeat the words to themselves (known in psychology as "rehearsal"), since the strategy based on forming mental images generally leads to better performance than mental rehearsal. But in reality, participants are using strategies in both cases—it is just that one is more effective than the other. So if we wish to understand people's cognitive performance, as well as performance differences between experimental conditions and participants, it is important to keep clearly in mind that a strategy is whatever approach a participant takes to performing a cognitive task, regardless of whether it leads to success or failure.

Heuristics, or algorithms, are particular types of strategy. A heuristic is a nonsystematic rule used to solve a problem, formulate a judgment, or make a decision. A heuristic does not necessarily lead to a correct response. For example, if participants are asked to estimate the number of demonstrators in a street, they might arrive at an estimate using the following heuristic: "the more space people occupy, the more demonstrators there are." An algorithm is a rule or a sequence of actions that, if it is correctly applied, necessarily leads to a correct response. For example, in an anagram solution task where a participant is asked to find a word consisting of the letters TSOLCE, it is possible to find a word such as CLOSET by systematically trying out the 720 possible combinations of these letters.

A strategy is not itself necessarily a mechanism or a procedure. Rather, a strategy comprises one or more procedures or mechanisms. In the current state of knowledge, psychologists use the terms "mechanism," "procedure," and "mental operations" as synonyms. In other words, a strategy is a series of mechanisms, procedures, or mental operations. By determining what strategies participants use, psychologists can understand how they accomplish different tasks and explain the performance differences between groups of participants and/or experimental conditions.

Awareness and strategy

Does a strategy have to be consciously used and verbalizable to be considered a strategy? Moreover, does it have to be executed deliberately?

In some domains and tasks, participants are aware of the strategies they use. In others, the strategies used are inaccessible to awareness. A strategy does not necessarily require awareness to be a strategy (see Dehaene, 2014, for examples of information-processing strategies which are used unconsciously). Participants are sometimes able to verbalize the strategies they apply—that is, name them and describe them. Other times, they simply cannot say what strategies they use. Again, participants do not have to be able to verbalize a strategy for this term to be applicable. There are no rules (yet) to systematically distinguish verbalizable strategies from nonverbalizable ones. Moreover, the links between awareness of a strategy and its verbalization have not yet been subjected to enough empirical scrutiny (see however Siegler & Stern, 1998). For now, then, we cannot say that the strategies that participants are able to verbalize are the same ones that they consciously implement, or that those they are unable to verbalize are applied unconsciously. In other words, we do not currently know whether awareness of a strategy is a necessary and sufficient condition for it to be verbalizable, although this may be the case. It is also not unlikely that participants' level of awareness of a strategy determines the level of verbalization that is available to them, so that the more consciously they apply a strategy, the better able they are to put it into words. At the least, to be able to verbalize a strategy, participants must activate a representation of it in working memory, this activation must reach a high enough level, and they must keep this representation active until the moment of verbalization. In other words, it is likely that the more highly activated a strategy is, and therefore the more it leads to a precise representation in working memory, the more accessible it will be to the participants, and the more able they will be to verbalize it—on condition that it be easily expressible in words, and that the participant have a rich enough vocabulary to verbalize it.

In some domains, participants deliberately behave strategically. That is, they intentionally, and perhaps consciously, choose to use a particular strategy (or subset of strategies) rather than another. This means that choices of what strategy to use in a given task can be entirely deliberate and intentional. In such cases, subjects are able to explain that they chose to use only two or three of the strategies they know to accomplish the task, and recognize that they could have used other strategies. In other domains, or in some particular tasks, strategy choices are not deliberate: That is, participants do not explicitly choose the strategies that they use. In this case, they are unable to say that they chose, say, to use only two of the five strategies that they know to accomplish the task that they just performed. They do not know how many strategies they used, nor are they able to say whether they used all of the strategies they know to perform the task. We currently know relatively little about the reasons for why participants choose to use only a single strategy or a subset of their repertoire of strategies, deliberately or not. They are likely related both to the nature of the strategies (conscious/unconscious; easy/difficult) and to participants' goal to optimize their performance by avoiding the heavy cognitive resource requirements of managing too many strategies. Here again, there may be a link between awareness and deliberate strategic behavior. It may be that the more deliberately participants choose their strategies, the more aware they are of those strategies and of their strategy choices.

In any case, further research is needed to understand the links between participants' awareness of a strategy they use and their abilities to verbalize it, on the one hand, and between awareness of strategy choices and their deliberateness, on the other hand. This research should answer important questions such as the following: What differentiates a conscious strategy from an unconscious strategy? Is awareness a necessary and sufficient condition for being able to reliably and accurately verbalize a strategy? Do levels of verbalization (i.e., the precision, validity, and reliability of participants' description of a strategy that they used) depend on their level of awareness of the strategies used on a given task? What are the links between how deliberately a set of strategies is applied in a task and the type or number of strategies used? Under what conditions (situation, participants, tasks, and cognitive domains) are strategies consciously and deliberately implemented (or not)?

Theoretical distinctions between strategies

What makes two strategies distinct from one another? This problem can be approached at two levels: Theoretical and empirical. At the theoretical level, two strategies differ in the number and/or the nature of the mental operations that they involve. Let us begin by using some abstract examples to look at how two strategies can differ (or not) in the number and/or the nature of the processes involved (the rest of the book will present many concrete, real examples).

Figure 2.1 illustrates two cases involving identical strategies, with the number and type of processes. The two strategies comprise three processes (a, b, c) in the first case and four processes (a, b, c, d) in the second case.

Figure 2.2 presents two cases where the two strategies differ in the number and nature of processes involved (Case 2a), or only in the number of processes (Case 2b). In Case 2a, the two strategies involve different numbers of processes, and have no processes in common. Strategy 1 consists of three processes (a, b, c), whereas Strategy 2 consists of four processes (d, e, f, g). None of these processes is common to the two strategies. This is thus a case of two radically different strategies. In Case 2b, the number of processes in the two strategies is not the same, although Strategy 2 includes all three of the processes (a, b, c) that make up

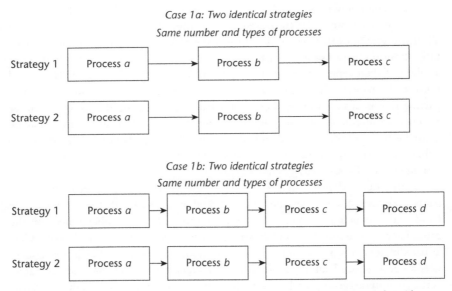

Case 1a: Two identical strategies
Same number and types of processes

Case 1b: Two identical strategies
Same number and types of processes

FIGURE 2.1 Description of two cases of strategies involving the same number (three in Case 1a and four in Case 1b) and types of processes. There is thus no valid reason to consider Strategies 1 and 2 to be distinct from one another in these cases.

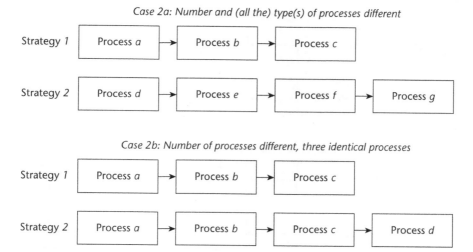

Case 2a: Number and (all the) type(s) of processes different

Case 2b: Number of processes different, three identical processes

FIGURE 2.2 Two cases of strategies which differ by virtue of the number and/or the nature of the processes that they include.

Strategy 1, as well as an additional process (*d*). The two strategies thus differ in the number of processes they include—specifically, the presence of an additional process in Strategy 2.

Figure 2.3 illustrates three cases with pairs of strategies which involve the same number of processes (i.e., each strategy includes three processes), some of which overlap and some of which differ. In Case 3a, the two strategies include two common processes (*a* and *b*) and one different process (*c* in Strategy 1 and *d* in Strategy 2). The two strategies in Case 3b include one common process (*a*) and two different processes (*b* and *c* in Strategy 1 and *d* and *e* in Strategy 2). In Case 3c, Strategy 1 consists of the processes *a*, *b*, and *c*, whereas Strategy 2 consists of processes *d*, *e*, and *f*.

Practically all cognitive tasks can be performed using multiple strategies. There are also variants of particular strategies. In different variants of a single strategy, the same processes are used, but in a different order. Figure 2.4 presents two examples, one with a strategy consisting of four processes, the other with a strategy consisting of five processes. As illustrated in this figure, each variant of a strategy is characterized by a particular distinct order of the processes involved. Thus, in the example of the strategy with four processes, the two variants are distinguished by the different order in which they feature processes *b* and *c* (whereas *a* and *d* are executed first and last, respectively, in both strategies). In the second case, the three examples of five-process strategies are distinguished by the order in which they feature processes *b*, *c* and *d*. Processes *c* and *d* are inverted in the second variant with respect to the first. In the third variant, it is processes *b* and *c* that are reversed.

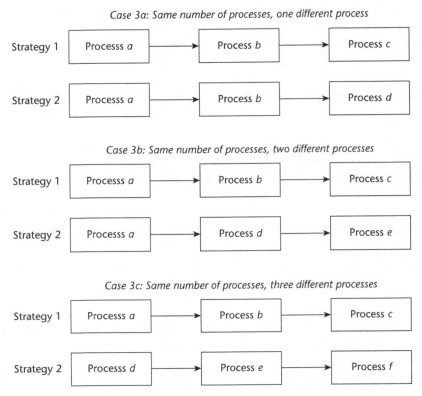

FIGURE 2.3 Cases of strategies involving the same number, but different types of processes.

These abstract cases illustrating the similarities and differences between two strategies can easily be generalized to cases of distinctions between three, four, or more strategies.

Empirical distinctions between strategies

On the empirical level, we are faced with two questions. First, how do we identify the strategies that participants use to perform a cognitive task? Second, what criteria should be applied to empirically validate a distinction between two (or more) strategies?

Empirical methods for studying strategies

One of the greatest difficulties researchers face when studying strategies is the difficulty of determining what strategies participants use when performing a cognitive task. Observing participants' behavior with the naked eye is not enough

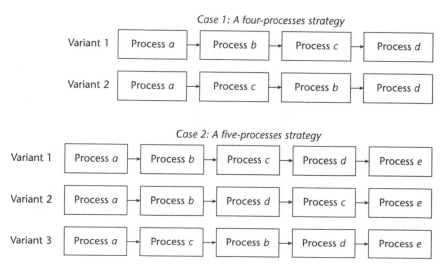

FIGURE 2.4   Variants of two strategies, one with four processes (Case 1), the other with five processes (Case 2).

to determine what strategies they are using. For example, just watching someone read does not allow us to see what reading strategies are used. Very often, the
only indicator we have of the strategies that participants use is their performance
(e.g., reading speed, number of words correctly recalled). In some domains, however,
there are external behavioral indicators that more directly reveal the strategies that
participants use. Broadly speaking, there are two families of methods for determining the strategy repertoire available for a particular cognitive task: Direct methods
and indirect methods.

Whenever possible, direct methods must be used to study cognitive strategies.
This minimizes the length of the inferential chain between participants' performance and its interpretation in terms of strategy. When researchers use direct
methods to study strategies, they try to collect as many external behavioral indicators of the strategies used as possible. These indicators include, notably, verbal
protocols (i.e., participants verbalize what they are doing), video recordings, and
other direct observation (e.g., gestures).

A study on differences between the strategies that young and older adults
use to perform the simple task of adding together two single-digit numbers
illustrates this direct approach. Geary and Wiley (1991) gave 60 young adults
(in their 20s) and 60 older adults (with a mean age of 70) 40 simple additions
to perform, such as 4 + 7 and 8 + 6. After each problem, they asked their participants to explain how they had done so (i.e., to explain the strategy they had
used), drawing on previous research which established the validity of this type
of verbal protocol. The analysis of their results revealed three broad categories
of strategies: Verbal counting, decomposition, and retrieval. In verbal counting,

participants initialized an internal counter at the value indicated by the larger operand, and then increased the counter incrementally in steps of size one or a number of times corresponding to the smaller operand (using the so-called minimum strategy) or the opposite (using the so-called maximum strategy). They thus calculated either $7 + 1 + 1 + 1 + 1$ or $4 + 1 + 1 + 1 + 1 + 1 + 1 + 1$ to solve $4 + 7$. In decomposition, they broke down one of the two operands into two numbers which they successively added to the other operand. For example, to calculate $4 + 7$, they calculated $4 + 4 + 3$. Finally, they also used direct retrieval of the result from long-term memory. Figure 2.5 shows the analysis of the different processes involved in each of these strategies.

Unfortunately, external behavioral evidence of participants' strategies is not always available. It is very often necessary to use indirect methods to determine what strategies they use. With indirect methods, the use of different strategies is inferred on the basis of how performance (i.e., speed and/or accuracy) varies with differences in parameters such as stimulus characteristics.

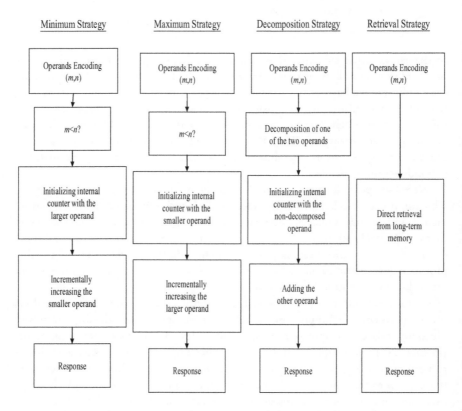

FIGURE 2.5   List of strategies (and their basic processes) used by participants to solve addition problems with pairs of single-digit numbers

The data published by Ashcraft and Battaglia (1978; see also Ashcraft & Stazyk, 1981; De Rammelaere, Stuyven, & Vandierendonck, 2001; Duverne & Lemaire, 2004, 2005; Duverne, Lemaire, & Vandierendonck, 2008; El Yagoubi, Lemaire, & Besson, 2003, 2005) illustrate this approach. Ashcraft and Battaglia asked their participants to verify arithmetic equations such as $8 \times 4 = 31$ (giving true–false responses). Along with true equations (e.g., $8 \times 5 = 40$), participants had to verify two types of false equations: "reasonable" (or small-split) false equations (such as $8 \times 4 = 31$) and "unreasonable" (or large-split) false equations (e.g., $8 \times 4 = 37$). The difference, or split, between the sum given and the true sum (32) was small in the first case (± 1 or 2) and large (± 5 or 6) in the second case. The participants were shown the problems and were instructed to respond as quickly and accurately as possible. They responded by depressing one of two response buttons located on a response box directly in front of them, one for true and one for false. As the data show (Figure 2.6a), the difference in verification times to the two types of false equalities can be interpreted in terms of a difference in strategies (consisting of distinct chains of processes; Figure 2.6b): An exhaustive verification strategy for the small-split equations, and a plausibility judgment strategy to verify the large-split equations.

One of the drawbacks of indirect methods is that, even if the data fit with an interpretation in terms of strategy differences, there are generally one or more alternative interpretations. For example, it could be that participants always used the exhaustive verification strategy, retrieving the exact answer and comparing it to the sum given in both types of false equations. In this case, the process of comparison might be executed more quickly for large-split answers than for small-split ones precisely because the distance between the proposed answer and the true answer is so much larger in the first case. It has long been known that, when participants have to compare pairs of numbers which are either far apart (e.g., which is larger, 2 or 9?) or close together (e.g., 7 and 9), they respond more quickly in the first case, as the comparison is easier to execute when the distance between the numbers is greater (e.g., Dehaene, Bossini, & Giraux, 1993; Moyer & Landauer, 1967). According to another interpretation of this effect (known as the distance effect), participants use the exhaustive verification strategy for both types of problems, but add an extra-verification process when they are faced with narrowly differing numbers. In this case, participants would indeed be using two different strategies for the two types of problems, but the difference would lie in the addition of an extra-verification process in one case, and not in the number and nature of processes, as suggested in Figure 2.6. To decide between multiple possible interpretations, then, further experiments are needed.

In the case of the distance effect, a number of researchers have provided further empirical evidence in favor of the strategy interpretation. For example, Duverne and Lemaire (2004) observed a significant Problem Size × Split interaction. The problem-size effect (i.e., participants respond more quickly to problems involving small numbers, such as $3 + 4$, than to those involving larger numbers, such as $8 + 9$) was greater for small-split problems (307 ms) than for large-split problems (144 ms). This is precisely the type of results that would be expected if participants used an exhaustive

(a)

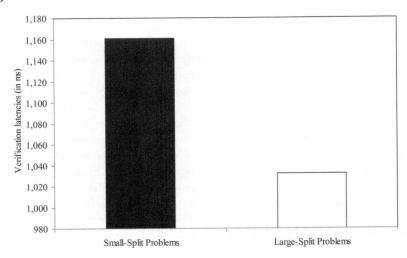

(b)

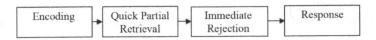

FIGURE 2.6 (a) Mean verification times for small–split and large–split false arithmetic equations (based on Ashcraft & Battaglia, 1978); (b) processes involved in the two strategies used to carry out these verifications.

verification strategy for small–split problems and an approximate verification strategy for large–split problems. Insofar as it takes longer to retrieve the exact result of large problems from long-term memory, the problem size effect should logically be greater in the condition where participants use a strategy based in large part on retrieval of the exact result (i.e., small–split problems) and be smaller (or even nonexistent) in the condition where the strategy used does not involve a retrieval process.

In conclusion, there are two families of methods for studying strategies: Direct methods and indirect methods. Because direct methods allow direct observation of the strategies that participants use through external behavioral indicators, they are less ambiguous and provide data which can be more clearly and less ambiguously interpreted in terms of strategies. They should thus be used whenever possible. However, it is not always possible to directly observe the strategies that participants use to complete a cognitive task. In this case, indirect methods based on performance differences between experimental conditions must be used instead. Data from such studies are subject to multiple interpretations. Further experiments are then needed to determine whether the results remain compatible with an interpretation in terms of strategy differences.

Distinctions between two (or more) strategies

In an experiment that we carried out in 2008, Laurence Arnaud and I (Lemaire & Arnaud, 2008) found that participants used nine different strategies to solve addition problems involving two two-digit numbers, such as 12 + 46. We proposed a distinction between columnar retrieval ([2 + 6] + [10 + 40]) followed by rounding down both operands to the closest decade ([10 + 40] + [2 + 6]). It may fairly be asked whether these are truly two different strategies, simply two variants of the same strategy, or even just a single strategy. This question is a general one, and it arises in practically all studies on strategies. What justifies distinguishing between two (or more) strategies? This is an important empirical question (i.e., one that cannot be answered without appropriate data). If we wish to characterize the exact sequence of mental operations that participants use to perform a cognitive task, we must indeed determine how many strategies they use, and what strategies these are.

Confidence in the presence of two distinct strategies is reinforced when four types of empirical evidence—experimental, developmental and/or differential, pathological, and neuroimaging—converge. Note that these four types of arguments are used whenever possible to confirm that any distinction between constructs, in psychology in general and in cognitive psychology in particular, is well founded (e.g., between short-term and long-term memory, declarative and procedural memory, automatic and controlled processes).

The first type of evidence used to distinguish two different strategies is the experimental evidence. This consists in an interaction between two factors. That is, a case where the effects of one factor on a measured variable (e.g., reaction time) differ depending on the values taken by another factor. Thus, strategy *a* and strategy *b* are different strategies if the performance difference between the two is modulated by another factor. For example, in sentence-picture verification tasks, Reichle, Carpenter, and Just (2000) found that the difference in verification time between a visual strategy and a verbal strategy depended on the type of statements that participants had to process (a Strategy × Statement Type interaction). The experimental setup used by Reichle et al. is illustrated in Figure 2.7. The participants saw a sentence displayed at the bottom of a computer screen (e.g., *It is true that the square is above the triangle*). They also saw two shapes (e.g., a star and a plus sign), one above the other. The participants' task was to indicate whether or not the sentence

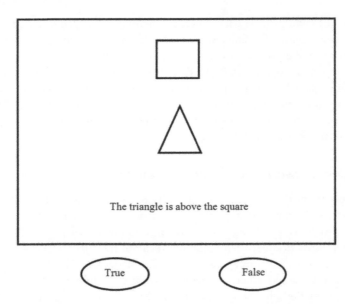

FIGURE 2.7 The experimental setup used by Reichle et al. (2000) to study strategy effects in a picture–sentence verification task. The participants' task was to say whether or not the sentence shown at the bottom of the screen correctly described the arrangement of the shapes.

correctly described the arrangement of the shapes. Two variables characterized the sentences presented at the bottom: Truth value (true vs. false), on the one hand, and polarity (affirmative vs. negative), on the other hand. For example, in Figure 2.7, *It is true that the square is above the triangle* is a true affirmative sentence; *It is true that the triangle is above the square* is a false affirmative sentence; *It is not true that the square is below the triangle* is a true negative sentence; and *It is not true that the square is above the triangle* is a false negative sentence.

Additionally, the participants were tested in two different experimental conditions. They were instructed to use a verbal strategy in one condition and a visual strategy in the other condition. In the verbal strategy condition they were given the following instructions:

> Quickly read each sentence when it is presented. Don't try to form a mental image of the objects in the sentence, but instead look at the sentence only long enough to remember it until the picture is presented. After the picture appears, decide whether or not the sentence that you are remembering describes the picture.

In the visual strategy condition, they were given the following instructions: "Carefully read each sentence and form a mental image of the objects in the sentence and their arrangement. After the picture appears, compare the picture to your mental image."

Verification times appear in Figure 2.8. The data show that, for each sentence type, participants performed faster when they used the visual strategy than when they used the verbal strategy. The verification time differences between visual and verbal strategies were largest for true negative sentences and smallest for true affirmative sentences. These data thus show that the strategies participants use in picture-sentence verification tasks affect their performance, and do so differently depending on the type of sentence they must process.

The second type of evidence for distinguishing two different strategies is the developmental evidence. According to the developmental (or differential) evidence, two strategies differ if they change differently with age (i.e., if they change at different rates as participants age). In other words, the performance difference between two groups of participants of different ages will differ for the two different strategies. For example, Robert Siegler and I (Siegler & Lemaire, 1997) compared times taken to solve multiplication problems on two two-digit numbers (e.g., 27 × 54) using either a mental calculation strategy or a calculator in young adults and adults above the age of 60. The data showed that, while all participants were faster with the calculator on average, the difference between mental calculation and using a calculator was larger in young participants than in older participants. Young people solved the problems using a calculator in an average of 4.3 seconds (vs. 8.4 seconds for older people), and 7.3 seconds with mental calculation (11.14 seconds for older adults). The percentage difference between the two strategies was higher for the young participants (41%) than for the older ones (25%).

At the level of individual differences, two strategies differ if two groups of individuals with different characteristics also show distinct performance differences between them. Many studies in a range of cognitive domains have observed such

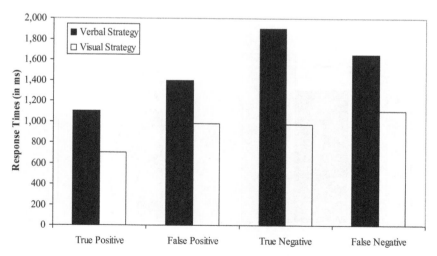

FIGURE 2.8 Picture-sentence verification times (in ms) for each strategy used and as a function of sentence type (based on Reichle et al., 2000).

individual differences. For example, in the United States, Delaney (1978) gave participants pairs of words to learn, the first in a foreign language and the second in English. The participants were tested in three conditions: A control condition (where they were given no instructions), a visual elaboration condition (where they were instructed to form an interactive mental image including the two words in each pair that they had to learn), and a verbal elaboration condition (where they had to make a sentence including the two words in each pair). The participants' language and visuospatial abilities were tested using independent neuropsychological tests (e.g., verbal fluency and synonym production tests for language abilities). The results of these tests were used to categorize participants as "high verbal fluency" or "high visualization/spatial ability." Delaney then examined the number of words correctly recalled in each condition according to the participants' individual profiles. A portion of the results is shown in Figure 2.9. The data clearly show that participants with lower language abilities performed better with the visual strategy than with the verbal strategy. The participants with stronger language abilities performed better with the verbal strategy than with the visual strategy. The opposite profile was found for participants with higher visuospatial abilities in comparison to those with lower visuospatial abilities.

The pathological evidence consists of a double dissociation. This is found when one patient (or more) presents a deficit in one strategy and not in another, while one other patient (or more) presents the opposite pattern (a deficit in the second strategy, and normal performance in the first). For example, in the domain of memory, researchers have isolated two types of strategies (or processes) for carrying out recognition tasks (see the review by Yonelinas, 2002). In a recognition task, participants first learn a series of items (words, images, faces, etc.). They then have to pick out which in a set of items presented

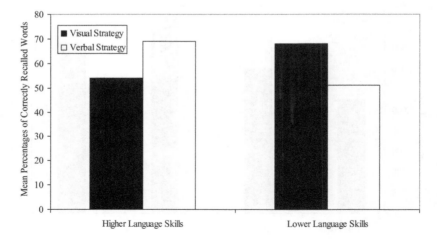

FIGURE 2.9   Percentages of words correctly recalled by participants with higher or lower language abilities by encoding strategy (based on Delaney, 1978).

later were in the list, and which are new. To do this, they can use either a so-called familiarity strategy or a recollection strategy. In a familiarity strategy, participants quickly and automatically establish an overall match between the memorized item and the judged item. In a recollection strategy, they attempt to retrieve one or more specific details, perceptual or contextual, from memory in order to check for a match. A number of neuropsychological studies have provided evidence of a double dissociation between these two strategies. For example, Barbeau et al. (2005) described one patient, FRG, who was unable to make normal use of the recollection strategy, whereas her use of the familiarity strategy was intact. At the age of 44, FRG had come down with herpetic encephalitis, which caused large lesions in her medial temporal lobe (i.e., complete destruction of the left medial temporal lobe, large lesions in the right hippocampus, but with some anterior subhippocampal structures such as the medial temporal pole and entorhinal and perirhinal cortex preserved). FRG had lost her memory. She failed massively at various recall tasks and at many recognition tasks. However, she was able to perform at a level similar to control participants on recognition tasks, which she could carry out using a familiarity strategy. For example, her performance on a task requiring her first to encode a series of faces and then to recognize them amongst a series of distractors was completely normal. She was able to distinguish the learned faces from the distractor faces because she was using a familiarity strategy, which allowed her to focus on the faces' perceptual features. However, she performed very poorly when the researchers asked her to carry out the same recognition task using words—a task that cannot be carried out using a familiarity strategy, only a recollection strategy.

Barbeau, Pariente, Felician, and Puel (2011) reported the opposite behavioral dissociation. They presented the case of JMG, who was comparable to FRG in many respects (age, IQ, a history of herpetic encephalitis), and who performed very poorly on visual recognition tasks but normally on a recognition task with verbal stimuli. In anatomical terms, like FRG, JMG's left medial temporal lobe had been almost completely destroyed. In contrast to FRG, however, his right hippocampus was preserved, whereas subhippocampal structures (i.e., temporal pole and entorhinal and perirhinal cortex) were either completely destroyed or severely damaged. This behavioral double dissociation, resulting from lesions of different brain areas, reinforces the distinction between a recognition strategy based on familiarity and a strategy based on recollection.

The neuroimaging evidence consists in different patterns of brain activation possibly reflecting the execution of different strategies. The study by Reichle et al. (2000) on picture-sentence verification cited above found that participants activated different brain networks when they were executing the verbal strategy than when they were using the visual strategy (Figure 2.10). Areas usually associated to language processing (e.g., Broca's area) were more active when the participants were using the verbal strategy than when they were using the visual strategy. Conversely, areas usually associated to visuospatial processing (e.g., parietal cortex) were more activated under the visual strategy than the verbal one. Interestingly, these activations

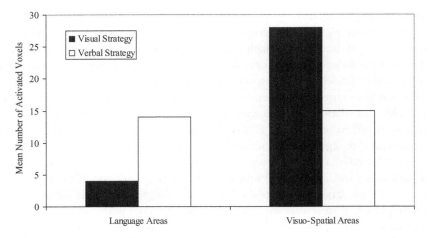

FIGURE 2.10 Number of voxels activated in language areas (e.g., superior temporal and inferior frontal areas) and in areas associated to visuospatial processing (e.g., left and right parietal cortex) when using the verbal strategy or the visual strategy (based on Reichle et al., 2000).

were modulated by individual differences. Individuals with stronger language abilities (as assessed using an independent test) tended to show less activation in Broca's area than those with lower language abilities when using the verbal strategy, and those with stronger visuospatial abilities showed less activation in left parietal cortex when using the visual strategy.

A further argument could theoretically be added to these four: The computational argument. According to this argument, if a model which postulates two strategies accounts better for the data than one that assumes a single strategy, the greater explanatory power of the former makes it preferable, even if it is less parsimonious.

Strategic variations and aging

Strategic variations

It is important to consider strategic variations when trying to explain performance differences between groups of individuals (e.g., young vs. older participants) or between different experimental situations or conditions (e.g., easy vs. difficult problems). Robert Siegler and I (Lemaire & Siegler, 1995) proposed a conceptual framework (which is illustrated in Figure 2.11) for distinguishing between several strategy dimensions (or variations). Robert Siegler and I applied this framework to children's development. I fruitfully extended its validity to cognitive aging (Lemaire, 2010).

An individual's *repertoire of strategies* characterizes the type and number of strategies used by an individual to perform a cognitive task. In any cognitive task, the first thing we want to know is which strategies the participants use. The *distribution of strategies* consists in the relative frequency at which participants use these different

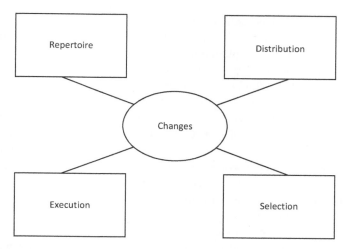

FIGURE 2.11 Conceptual framework proposed by Lemaire and Siegler (1995; Lemaire, 2010) and its distinction between four different strategy dimensions.

strategies. What percentage of the time do they use each strategy? The question of *strategy execution* is about how an individual implements a given strategy, or the performance levels (in terms of speed and accuracy) associated to each strategy. Finally, there are the *strategy choices* that individuals make when solving any given problem. Here the question is to identify the predictors of the use of the different strategies, in order to understand what mechanisms lead the individual to use one or another strategy to solve any given problem.

Aging and strategic variations

The conceptual framework proposed by Lemaire and Siegler (1995; Lemaire, 2010) is useful for posing the question of strategic variations with age. The general question is whether changes in cognitive performance during aging are associated to the strategies used by young and older participants. This question can be divided into several subquestions corresponding to the different strategy dimensions in Lemaire and Siegler's conceptual framework.

The first of these is the question of whether individuals' repertoire of strategies changes during aging. In other words, one of the very first questions that researchers who are trying to understand performance differences between young and older participants must ask is the question of strategy repertoire. Did the two groups of participants complete the task in the same way—that is, using the same number of strategies, and in fact the same set of strategies (or the same type of strategies)? If the performance differences between young and older participants are associated to differences in their repertoires of strategies, it is likely not necessary to appeal to another factor to explain performance differences, such as cognitive slowing (unless the slowing is responsible for a difference in repertoire). The next question is whether young and older participants use each of the available strategies a similar proportion of the time. It is entirely possible, for example, that older participants use strategies which are difficult to implement more often than easier strategies, and that young adults do the opposite. This would necessarily lead to a performance disadvantage for older adults, even if the two groups use the same strategies.

The other two dimensions which must be compared between young and older participants are strategy execution and choices. For execution, the question is whether older adults are as efficient at using the available strategies as young adults. If not, then even if the two groups use the same strategies in the same proportions, their performance will differ as a result. Finally, young and older participants can differ in how they choose which strategy to use. That is, the type of problems to which each of the two groups applies each strategy may differ. If older adults do not systematically use the best strategy for each problem (or do so less often than younger adults), this is enough for them to show worse performance, even if the two groups use the same strategies in similar proportions and with equivalent efficiency.

In the following chapters, I will attempt to answer these questions. Each of the answers will contribute to answering the general question: Are there strategic variations associated to aging? We will survey data from the literature, asking the questions of whether, on different tasks and in different cognitive domains, young and older adults use the same repertoire of strategies, whether they make use of each of them a comparable proportion of the time and with similar efficiency, and whether they are equally likely to choose the best strategy for each problem. In doing so, we will look at data from domains as diverse as attention, memory, problem solving, reasoning, decision making, and language processing. This will allow us to understand why in some studies, researchers have observed strategic variations during aging, while studies in other domains—or even studies from the same domains by the same researchers—have failed to find such strategic variations. This lack of strategic variations is due as much to failure to study them intentionally as to the fact that, sometimes, young and older adults are extremely similar in terms of strategic variations.

After this survey, it will be possible to set out the general characteristics of the domains of cognition and conditions where aging is accompanied by strategic variations, as well as those of the cases where young and older adults show similar strategic variations. It will also illustrate the interest of studying cognitive aging from a strategy perspective. This approach has a number of merits. For one thing, it allows us to more accurately describe how cognitive performance changes with age (by determining what deteriorates and what remains stable with age) and inter-individual differences in those changes (or how certain older people age better than others, in one or more domains). It also offers an interesting pathway to uncovering the compensation mechanisms that some older people sometimes use in certain cognitive domains to deal with the consequences of aging. More generally, the strategy perspective offers a mechanistic explanation for changes in cognitive performance during aging. The findings discussed in the chapters that follow amply illustrate these merits of the strategy approach advocated in this book.

3

AGING AND STRATEGY REPERTOIRE

Chapter outline

The strategy repertoire issue concerns how participants go about performing cognitive tasks. In other words, it is a matter of finding out what sequence of mental operations they perform in order to achieve a cognitive goal. This is a fundamental question in cognitive psychology. In fact, it is probably *the* fundamental question in cognitive psychology, which is common to all researchers regardless of their specialty. It is against the background of this general question that psychologists studying cognitive aging seek to determine whether our strategy repertoire changes as we age. A change in strategy repertoire with age can mean using different strategies. It can also mean using fewer (or more) different strategies with age. The findings discussed in this chapter were gathered in order to determine whether, as we age, we use a larger (or smaller) number of strategies, and/or a different set of strategies, to perform a given cognitive task. The answers to these questions have important implications on both the theoretical level and the empirical level. On the theoretical level, the observation of age-related differences in strategies could invalidate a "quantitative" approach to aging. This is an approach which postulates (explicitly or implicitly) that differences between young and older adults can be understood in terms of a quantitative decrease in one or more cognitive resources (e.g., working memory, information-processing speed, inhibition). For example, the observation that older adults use slower strategies than young adults to perform a cognitive task would suggest that age-related differences in performance may not be explained by cognitive slowing, as postulated by processing-speed theories of aging (e.g., Cerella, 1985; Salthouse, 1996). These differences could instead be simply due to the fact that young and older adults carry out different mental operations, and that the operations older people perform are slower. If this is true, the question then becomes whether the differences in the information-processing modes of young and older people are a necessary and sufficient source of aging-related differences in cognitive performance. In this case, researchers' task is to try and identify the origins of these age-related qualitative differences in information processing. In reality, as we will see, these two approaches to cognitive aging, qualitative and quantitative, are complementary. It is possible, notably, that strategy changes themselves result at least partly from age-related quantitative changes in the cognitive system. Before exploring this point, we will first look at whether there are in fact differences between the strategy repertoires of young and older adults.

Directly observing strategies: The example of arithmetic

A number of studies have revealed that, in certain cognitive tasks, older people tend to use fewer and/or different strategies than young people.

Laurence Arnaud and I (Lemaire & Arnaud, 2008) carried out a study where we sought to determine how young and older participants go about solving addition problems with two two-digit numbers, such as 23 + 48. We discovered that young and older participants use nine strategies (Table 3.1) to solve these problems. Suzanne Hodzik and I (Hodzik & Lemaire, 2011) later replicated these results. An interesting point about these two studies is that, at the group level, we found the same repertoire of nine strategies in both young and older adults. The two age groups were thus familiar with all nine strategies. But when we counted the number of strategies that each individual used to solve the problems that they were given, we found that, while young people used an average of five out of the nine available strategies, older people used an average of only three. It was as if,

TABLE 3.1 List of strategies used by young and older participants to solve addition problems with two two-digit numbers (based on Lemaire & Arnaud, 2008)

Strategy	Example (12 + 46)
1 Rounding the first operand down to the nearest decade	(10 + 46) + 2
2 Rounding the second operand down to the nearest decade	(12 + 40) + 6
3 Rounding both operands down to the nearest decades	(10 + 40) + (2 + 6)
4 Columnar retrieval	(2 + 6) + (10 + 40)
5 Rounding the first operand up to the nearest decade	(20 + 46) − 8
6 Rounding the second operand up to the nearest decade	(12 + 50) − 4
7 Rounding both operands up to the nearest decades	(20 + 50) − 8 − 4
8 Borrowing units	18 + 40
9 Direct retrieval from memory	58

while individuals in both age groups were familiar with all nine available strategies, older adults deliberately chose to use fewer of them than young adults.

This difference in the size of the strategy repertoire of young and older adults has been observed in other arithmetic problem-solving tasks, both in cases where participants' strategies can be observed directly and in cases where they must be inferred on the basis of performance. For example, Geary and Lin (1998) observed that, in solving complex subtraction problems (such as 53 − 9), young participants used four strategies, whereas older participants used only one. Young participants used: (1) Counting down (e.g., to calculate 24 − 3, participants counted 24, 23, 22, 21); (2) columnar retrieval (e.g., to calculate 24 − 3, participants calculated 4 − 3 = 1, 2 − 0 = 2, and thus 21), (3) decomposition (e.g., to calculate 35 − 9, participants calculated 35 − 10 = 25; 10 − 9 = 1; 25 + 1 = 26); and (4) rule strategy (i.e., to calculate 35 − 9, participants did the following: 35 − 10 = 25; 10 − 9 = 1; 25 + 1 = 26). Older participants used only columnar retrieval to solve all the problems.

Indirectly observing differences in strategy repertoire: The example of arithmetic

Arithmetic is a cognitive domain that offers good opportunities to study strategy variations in human cognition, as well as age-related differences in these variations. Notably, the strategies used in certain arithmetic tasks can be observed directly, as in the studies cited above, although in others they cannot. Studying strategies in arithmetic thus often requires the use of indirect methods, as in many other cognitive domains. One example is a study that Sandrine Duverne and I (Duverne & Lemaire, 2004) carried out on age-related differences in strategy repertoire. We used a task where participants' strategies had to be inferred on the basis of how their performance was affected by variations in certain parameters (such as stimulus characteristics). Specifically, we asked participants between the ages of 20 and 80 years to verify arithmetic inequalities which were either simple (e.g., 3 + 8 < 12. Yes/No?) or complex (157 + 176 < 334). The critical question was the effect of the difference (or "split") between the suggested answer and the correct answer. The split was small (e.g., 3 + 8 < 12; 157 + 176 < 334) in half of the problems and large in the other problems (e.g., 3 + 8 < 19; 157 + 176 < 397). The participants were instructed to respond as quickly as possible without making any mistakes. Figure 3.1 shows the verification times for complex inequalities. The data revealed significant effects of split (i.e., solution times for large-split problems < solution times for small-split problems) in young participants (between ages 20 and 40) and middle-aged participants (between ages 40 and 65), but no difference in solution times between the two types of problems in older participants (above age 65).

In the literature on arithmetic problem solving, the split effect is generally interpreted as a result of the use of two different types of strategies (e.g., Ashcraft & Battaglia, 1978; Duverne & Lemaire, 2004; Duverne, Lemaire, & Vandierendonck, 2008). According to this strategy interpretation, the participants use an exhaustive verification strategy to verify small-split inequalities and a plausibility-checking

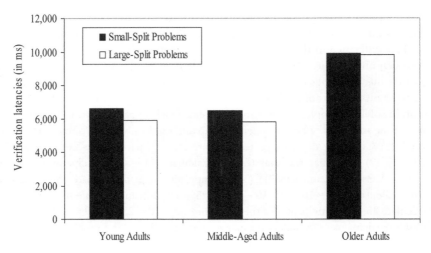

FIGURE 3.1 Verification times for complex arithmetic inequalities (data from Duverne & Lemaire, 2004). Participants had to indicate whether the proposed inequalities were true or false. The inequalities were either small-split problems (i.e., the difference between the proposed answer and the correct answer was small; e.g., 157 + 176 < 334) or large-split problems; e.g., 157 + 176 < 397). These data show that young and middle-aged participants responded more quickly to large-split problems than to small-split problems (because they used a rapid plausibility-checking strategy on the former and an exhaustive verification strategy on the latter), whereas older adults took the same amount of time with both types of problems (likely because they used the same slow exhaustive verification strategy for both types of problems).

strategy to verify large-split inequalities. The exhaustive verification strategy is thought to consist of the following processes: Encoding of the operands and the proposed answer, calculation of the correct answer, comparison of the proposed answer and the calculated correct answer, decision (Yes/No?), and responding (pressing the corresponding key on the computer). For example, when their task is to verify an inequality such as 8 + 3 < 12, participants would first encode 8, 3, and 12. They would then calculate the exact sum of 8 and 3 (11); compare the calculated sum and the proposed sum (11 and 12); decide whether, as the problem suggests, 11 < 12; and give their (positive) response by pressing on the corresponding key on the keyboard (or the corresponding button on a response box). In contrast, when faced with inequalities such as 8 + 3 < 19, the participants would know very quickly (without needing to complete the process of retrieving the sum 8 + 3 = 11 from memory) that 19 is too far from the correct response to be plausible. Consequently, they would quickly accept the inequality without going through the whole chain of processes involved in verifying small-split problems. They likely knew the answer on the basis of the automatic activation of a set of information about the true result of 8 + 3. Hence the finding of substantially shorter reaction times for large-split problems than for small-split problems.

The results of Duverne and Lemaire (2004) suggested that young and middle-aged adults did indeed use two different strategies, one for each type of problem. Older adults, however, seemed to use only one strategy, the exhaustive verification strategy, to verify the two types of inequalities. Thus far, it has not yet been clearly established whether the disappearance of the split effect in older adults results from the loss of the plausibility-checking strategy from their strategy repertoire (which seems unlikely), or whether this strategy is available to them but they do not use it. It could be, moreover, that it is available to older adults and they in fact use it. However, lacking confidence in their answer, older adults are driven to use an additional double verification strategy (for example, calculating the precise answer and verifying that this calculation leads to the same response as the plausibility-checking strategy). Note, however, that while such an interpretation is possible, it was invalidated in young adults by Duverne et al. (2008), who found a Problem Difficulty × Split interaction in this age group. That is, participants took longer to verify problems with larger numbers (e.g., 9 + 7) than those with smaller numbers (e.g., 3 + 4) only if splits between proposed and correct answers were small, but they took the same amount of time for small and large problems when splits were large. This result is consistent with the strategy hypothesis (i.e., the use of different strategies with problems involving smaller and larger numbers), and inconsistent with the hypothesis of the use of a double verification process with large-split problems. The data are inconsistent with the latter interpretation because calculating the exact answer (or directly retrieving it from memory) takes longer with larger problems (see, e.g., Zbrodoff & Logan, 2005, for a review on problem-size effects in arithmetic), and latencies should be affected by problem size when participants use retrieval or the exact calculation of the answer. This is what they in fact do with small-split problems. With large-split problems, however, participants do not need to retrieve (or calculate) the exact answer (or carry the process of calculation/retrieval to conclusion), insofar as they can quickly determine that the proposed answer is false based on a rapid judgment of its plausibility. As a result, with a large split, they take the same amount of time to respond to large and small problems.

Note that the presence or absence of differences in strategy repertoire does not necessarily depend on the domain or the task studied. Thus, in arithmetic problem verification tasks, Duverne and Lemaire (2004, 2005) and others (e.g., Allen, Ashcraft, & Weber, 1992; Allen, Smith, Jerge, & Vires-Collins, 1997; Allen et al., 2005; Duverne, Lemaire, & Michel, 2003) have observed differences in strategy repertoire between young and older adults. But Hinault, Tiberghien, and Lemaire (2015) recently found that young and older participants sometimes use the same strategies in the same type of verification task. The objective of Hinault et al.'s study was to determine whether older participants use strategies based on checking for violations of arithmetic rules. Earlier studies had shown that young adults use these types of strategies, such as the five-rule and parity-rule violation-checking strategies (Hinault, Dufau, & Lemaire, 2014; Krueger & Hallford, 1984; Krueger, 1986;

Lemaire & Fayol, 1995; Lemaire & Reder, 1999; Masse & Lemaire, 2001). According to the five rule, the products of problems including five as an operand must end with either five or zero (e.g., $5 \times 14 = 60$; $5 \times 17 = 85$). According to the parity rule, to be true, a product must be even, if either of its multipliers is even; otherwise, it must be odd (e.g., $4 \times 18 = 72$; $3 \times 18 = 54$; $3 \times 17 = 51$). Previous works had shown that participants respond more quickly when a proposed answer is wrong and violates a rule than when it is wrong but respects the rule. Thus, participants are quicker to respond that 69 is not the result of 5×13 than they are to respond that 60 is the wrong answer. They are able to quickly determine that 69 cannot be the correct product of a multiplication including 5 as an operand without having to calculate the exact product. In contrast, because 60 is a potentially correct product of 5 and another number, the participants will calculate the exact product of 5×13 (65), compare it to 60, and decide that the proposed answer is wrong. In other words, they use a rapid five-rule violation-checking strategy to reject $5 \times 13 = 69$, and a slower exhaustive verification strategy to reject $5 \times 13 = 60$. The latter strategy, which involves a larger number of processes, is slower.

In another example, participants are quicker to respond that $7 \times 13 = 92$ is false (since 92 violates the parity rule) than to respond that $7 \times 13 = 93$ is false (since 93 respects the parity rule), all else being equal. In other words, participants are quicker to reject $7 \times 13 = 92$ than $7 \times 13 = 93$ because they use a parity-rule violation-checking strategy in the first case and an exhaustive verification strategy in the second case. Note that previous studies have shown that the use of the parity rule is unconscious (less than 5% of participants report using it), whereas the use of the five rule is conscious (more than 95% of participants report using it).

The goal of Hinault and collaborators (2015) was to determine whether older participants use five-rule and parity-rule violation-checking strategies. We also wanted to find out whether young and older adults manage to combine the two strategies into a single, faster strategy. To do this, they gave young and older participants a verification task. The problems were either true or false, and either included five as an operand ("five problems") or did not ("nonfive problems"). More specifically, they examined participants' performance on the four types of false-five problems. To wit: (1) problems involving no rule violation (e.g., $5 \times 26 = 140$); (2) problems where only the parity rule was violated, but the five rule was respected (e.g., $5 \times 12 = 65$); (3) problems where only the five rule was violated, but not the parity rule (e.g., $5 \times 32 = 162$); and (4) problems violating both the five rule and the parity rule (e.g., $5 \times 31 = 158$). The mean verification times are shown in Figure 3.2. The data revealed that both young and older adults took less time to verify problems that violated both rules than for those that violated only the five rule, which in turn they verified more quickly than problems that violated only the parity rule. The longest times were for problems that violated no rule. This suggests that both groups of participants used different verification strategies for the different types of problems. More specifically, both young and older participants used the parity-rule violation-checking strategy for problems that violated only the parity rule, the five-rule violation-checking strategy for those that violated only the five

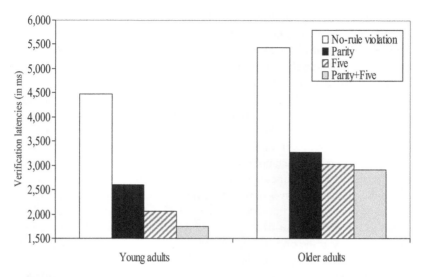

FIGURE 3.2 Problem verification times for problems with no arithmetic rule violations, problems violating the parity rule, problems violating the five rule, and problems violating both rules, in young and older participants (data from Hinault et al., 2015). These data show that the two groups of participants used arithmetic-rule violation-checking strategies for problems that violate either or both of these rules, and an exhaustive verification strategy to reject false-five problems which violated no rule.

rule, and a combination of the two strategies for problems that violated both rules. This strategy combination could take the following form: "In a problem including five as an operand, the correct product is even if the other operand is even and odd if the other operand is odd" (i.e., 5 × even operand = even product; 5 × odd operand = odd product). For problems with no rule violations, participants likely used an exhaustive verification strategy. Note that the speed advantage with problems involving violations of both rules was slightly smaller in older participants than in young participants. It is impossible to say on the basis of these data whether this difference was a result of older participants making less frequent and/or systematic use of the strategy combination, and/or because they were less efficient in executing the strategy. This is the drawback of indirect methods: They cannot tell us what particular strategy dimension differentiates young and older participants.

Indirectly observing differences in strategy repertoire in other cognitive domains

In many domains of cognition, strategies cannot be directly observed, but must be inferred on the basis of behavioral (or other) indicators. Thus, in the sensorimotor domain, for example, participants' performance can be used to infer the strategies they use and, on that basis, to determine whether young and older participants make use of the same strategy repertoire. In a recent study, Poletti, Sleimen-Malkoun, Temprado, and Lemaire (2015) asked participants to perform a Fitts' aiming task (often used to study sensorimotor mechanisms) and the effect of age in this domain.

In this task, participants have to move a stylus from a starting point to a target location (see Figure 3.3 for an illustration of the experimental setup). The system records the movement of the stylus, making it possible to determine all the characteristics of the movement (speed, final stopping point, corrections, etc.) and to study these characteristics in different groups of participants as a function of various parameters (e.g., distance between the starting point and the target; size of the target). On the basis of a kinematic analysis of this movement (e.g., calculation of the first and second derivatives of the movement on the basis of speed), Poletti et al. were able to determine that, across all trials, their participants used four different strategies to reach the target (see Figure 3.4 for an illustration of these strategies). The first strategy was the one-shot strategy—that is, an approach where participants spent equal amounts of time accelerating and decelerating. In the second strategy, the overshoot strategy, participants first went past the target and then made a small corrective movement in the opposite direction to reach it. In the third strategy, the undershoot strategy, participants made an initial movement that ended just short of the target, and then a second accelerated movement to reach it. The fourth strategy was the progressive deceleration strategy. It consisted in a brief initial acceleration followed by a long deceleration all the way to the target, with a slowing of the movement as the stylus came close to the target.

Poletti et al.'s data showed that, at the group level, both young and older participants used these four strategies. At the individual level, however, on average, each older individual used fewer strategies than each young individual. Across all items, no individual, young or older, exclusively used a single strategy to perform the Fitts' task: Four older adults used two strategies, six young and six older individuals used three strategies, and three young people and one older person used all four strategies. In other words, young adults displayed a larger strategy repertoire than older adults, and more young adults used larger numbers of strategies.

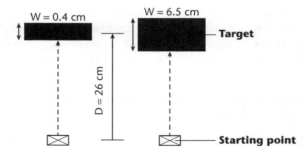

FIGURE 3.3 Setup used by Poletti et al. (2015) to study strategy differences between young and older people in a Fitts' aiming task.

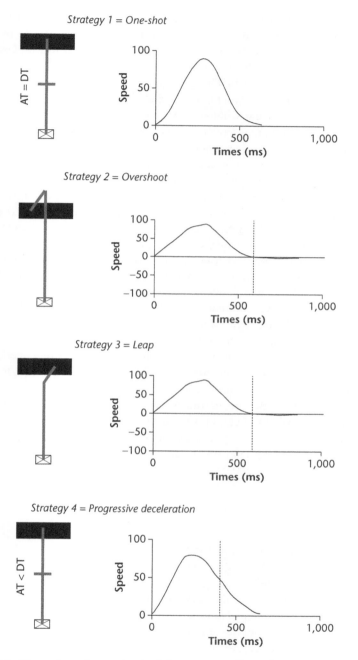

FIGURE 3.4 Illustration of strategies (and the corresponding velocity curves) used by young and older participants to reach a target in a Fitts' aiming task (based on Poletti et al., 2015). AT, acceleration time; DT, deceleration time; the dotted line indicates a transition in the velocity curve which distinguishes the different strategies.

Elizabeth Stine-Morrow and her collaborators have collected equivalent data on age-related differences in strategy repertoires in reading and language processing (e.g., Shake, Noh, & Stine-Morrow, 2009; Stine, 1990; Stine-Morrow, Loveless, & Soederberg, 1996; Stine-Morrow, Miller, & Hertzog, 2006; Stine-Morrow, Shake, Miles, Lee, & McConkie, 2010). The participants were informed that their memory of the content of the texts would be tested after they read them. The texts were presented with the moving-window technique. That is, they were presented in a blurred form on a computer screen. The word that the participant was fixating on at a given moment was made temporarily sharp, and then was blurred again as the participant's gaze shifted to the next word, which itself became clear, and so on as participants moved through the text. The times taken by young and older participants to read each word were recorded. Using statistical regression techniques, the authors then assessed the effects of several linguistic parameters (e.g., word frequency, propositional boundaries, line breaks) on reading times. When they compared the reading times of young and older participants who scored well on the recall test, they discovered that reading times were influenced by different factors in the two groups. In young people, reading was strongly influenced by the characteristics of words (such as frequency), and by the introduction of new concepts, whereas older people were more influenced by contextual factors (such as the ends of propositions and paragraphs). These data suggest an important age-related difference in how participants read texts, and particularly in how they distribute their attentional resources at encoding in order to optimize their later recall performance (see Kail, Lemaire, & Lecacheur, 2012, and Wotschack & Kliegl, 2013, for similar data from sentence comprehension tasks).

Let us note, finally, that many studies have also shown that older participants' knowledge of available strategies is similar to that of young participants in many other domains, such as memory (e.g., Dixon & Hultsch, 1983; Hertzog & Hultsch, 2000; Loewen, Shaw, & Craik, 1990), decision making (e.g., Johnson, 1990; Mata, Schooler, & Rieskamp, 2007), and reasoning (e.g., Hartley, 1986; Hartley & Anderson, 1983).

Conclusions

In this chapter, we have seen that there can sometimes be age-related differences in strategy repertoire. When these differences exist, they are often manifested by older people's use of fewer strategies than young people. To my knowledge, the opposite, older people using more different strategies than young people, has never been observed. These differences in strategy repertoire have been established both in domains where strategies can be directly observed and in domains where they are inferred on the basis of performance. These domains are highly varied (Table 3.2). They run from reading and sentence comprehension to problem solving, episodic memory, and even (more recently) sensorimotor performance. Sometimes, within a single domain—as in arithmetic—differences in the strategy repertoires of young and older adults have been reported for some tasks, while no differences have been

TABLE 3.2 A nonexhaustive list of studies of studies showing change in strategy repertoire during aging

Cognitive domain	Type of task used	Study
Sensorimotor performance	Fitts' task	Bennett, Elliott, & Rodacki, 2012; Elliot et al., 2010; Fradet, Lee, & Dounskaia, 2008; Ketcham, Seidler, Van Gemmert, & Stelmach, 2002; Poletti et al., 2015; Wisleder & Dounskaia, 2007;
Selective visual attention	Target detection with spatial cuing	Folk & Hoyer, 1992; McCalley, Bouwhuis, & Juola, 1995
Divided attention	Two near-simultaneous choice reaction time tasks	Maquestiaux, Didierjean, Ruthruff, Chauvel, & Hartley, 2013
Numerical cognition	Complex addition problem-solving tasks	Hodzik & Lemaire, 2011; Lemaire & Arnaud, 2008
	Problem verification tasks	Allen et al., 1992, 1997, 2005;
	Complex subtraction problem-solving tasks	Duverne & Lemaire, 2004
		Geary & Lin, 1998
Episodic memory	Source memory tasks	Kuhlmann & Touron, 2012
	Paired associates learning tasks	Naveh-Benjamin, Brav, & Levy, 2007
Decision making	Variable-reward card selection tasks	Worthy & Maddox, 2012
	Mars farming task	Cooper, Worthy, Gorlick, & Maddox, 2013
	Card choice tasks	Besedes, Deck, Sarangi, & Shor (2012)
	Purchase decision tasks	Mata & Nunes, 2010
	Apartment and bank choice tasks	Queen & Hess, 2010
Spatial reasoning	Kohs cubes	Rozencwajg et al., 2005

found for other tasks. It is important to note that young and older adults have never been found to differ in strategy repertoire in the sense of using radically different strategies. The various strategies found in the strategy repertoire of young people do not seem to disappear with age; neither do new ones seem to emerge. It seems that older adults continue to have these strategies in their repertoire, but simply do not use a portion of them. Theoretically, it is not beyond the realm of possibility that older people perform some cognitive tasks using strategies which do not exist in young people. Likewise, it is conceivable that in some tasks, older people use a larger number of strategies than young people. These possibilities require further empirical investigations. Perhaps, for example, ingenious experimental designs might be used that incite older people to use more strategies, or even novel strategies.

The observation of change in strategy repertoire with age has important general consequences, both on the theoretical level and on the empirical level. First of all, it means that it is important to determine how young and older participants perform any given cognitive task. This is one of the first things to be done in order then to be able to explain age-related differences (or similarities) in cognitive performance. These differences could be due to change in information-processing modes with aging, wherein older people process information differently than young people as they attempt to accomplish the tasks that they are given. If, in doing so, older people use strategies which are more difficult to execute (and thus slower) than young people, it is not surprising that they are slower overall. It is important also to try and determine the origins of these differences in strategy repertoire, once it has been established that older people's use of a smaller number of strategies does not result from the disappearance of unused strategies with age. If older people use a smaller number of strategies, which are also more difficult to execute, then they will present a different cognitive profile than if they use fewer but easier-to-execute strategies. Both of these cases have been reported in the literature. In other words, determining what strategy repertoire young and older adults respectively use to perform a cognitive task allows us to achieve the first objective of the psychology of cognitive aging: To characterize the changes in information-processing modes during aging, and thereby determine whether there are qualitative differences in human cognition with aging.

Obviously, just because differences in strategy repertoire have been observed in many domains does not mean that they exist in all domains, or in all tasks within a given domain. In domains where no age-related differences in strategy repertoire are found, but performance differences between young and older participants are nonetheless observed, this means that information-processing modes do not explain these differences. They may result from other strategy dimensions, such as strategy distribution, execution, and selection, as we will see in the chapters that follow.

4

AGING AND STRATEGY DISTRIBUTION

Chapter outline

Equivalent strategy distributions in young and older adults

Differing strategy distributions in young and older adults

Modulation of age-related differences in strategy distributions

Conclusions

Whether or not participants use the same number and types of strategies, they can differ in their strategy distribution. The strategy distributions of two groups of individuals (e.g., young vs. older adults) can be compared through either the proportion of individuals who use each strategy, or the percentage of items on which each individual uses each of the available strategies. The first (the proportion of individuals using a given strategy) is examined by attempting to determine what strategy each individual used overall. This is assessed by probing the participant at the end of the experiment (using off-line verbal protocols). The proportion of individuals using a given strategy is also examined when participants are characterized on the basis of the strategy that they mainly used, as inferred from other behavioral indicators. Strategy distributions are also compared on the basis of mean percentages of items for which each strategy is used. This can be determined with on-line verbal protocols for each item. In on-line verbal protocols, participants are instructed to verbalize what they are doing as they perform a task, or asked what strategy they used after each item. A few conditions must be met for the latter approach to be possible: The collection of verbal protocols should not interfere with participants' performance or change their approach to the task; participants must be able to verbalize the strategy they used; and participants must provide valid and reliable verbalizations of the strategies they used. In this chapter, we will consider a variety of findings related to whether aging leads to changes in strategy distributions.

Equivalent strategy distributions in young and older adults

The results of a number of studies seem to suggest that, in some domains and for some tasks, strategy distribution does not vary with age. In arithmetic problem solving, for example, Geary and Lin (1998) observed that, when solving simple subtraction problems (e.g., 9 − 3), young and older participants used the addition reference and direct memory retrieval strategies the same proportions of the time. Young adults used the addition reference strategy (i.e., for 9 − 3, they referred to the corresponding addition, 6 + 3 = 9) on 3% of problems (2% for older adults), while young and older adults directly retrieved the answer from memory on 97% and 98% of problems respectively (see Geary, Frensch, & Wiley, 1993, for similar results with more complex subtractions, such as 36 − 9).

In a series of experiments aimed at determining whether young and older participants use the same strategies to encode information in episodic memory, Dunlosky and Hertzog (1998) asked participants to learn word pairs (cue–target) that were either semantically related (such as *king–crown*) or not (such as *arm–market*). The participants were shown 60 word pairs for 4 or 8 seconds each, and had to learn them in order to perform a later recall test. After each word pair, the participants had to indicate what strategy they had used to encode it. On the recall task, after encoding, the cue words were presented again, and participants had to recall the associated target words. The results of this study confirmed the classical effect of age on recall performance, with young participants recalling significantly more words than older participants. When the authors looked at how frequently each of the two age groups used the available strategies (Figure 4.1), they found that young and older adults had similar strategy distributions. Both groups most often used mental imagery and sentence generation, followed by mental repetition, and finally other strategies or no strategy at all. They found no significant differences between young and older adults in the proportion of use of each strategy (see also Dunlosky & Hertzog, 2001; Hertzog & Hultsch, 2000; Loewen, Shaw, & Craik, 1990).

Kuhlmann and Touron (2012) recently observed age-related differences in strategy distributions on source memory tasks. In these tasks, participants heard words spoken either by a male voice or a female voice. Their task was not only to learn the words, but to remember their source (i.e., was this word spoken by a man's voice or a woman's voice?). In another type of source memory task, participants saw words in either italic or bold type. Their task was to learn not only the words but the font (bold or italic) that they were shown in. Kuhlmann and Touron gave this task to 22 young adults and 20 older adults. Their participants had to read 50 words on a computer screen, half of which were in bold type, and the other half in italics. After this encoding phase, the participants were shown the words again and had to indicate which of the proposed strategies (i.e., imagery, sentence generation, and mental repetition, other strategy, no strategy) they had used to encode the item. Then, during the recall phase, the participants were shown 100 words, the 50 words from the encoding phase and 50 new words. They first had to say whether each

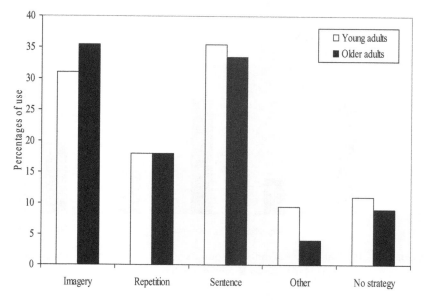

FIGURE 4.1 Young and older participants' percentage use of different encoding strategies to encode word pairs (data from Dunlosky & Hertzog, 1998). The results show that young and older adults were similar in using the creation of mental images and sentences more frequently, and other strategies less frequently.

word was old (i.e., it had been presented in the encoding phase) or new. For each word they said was old, they had to specify whether it had been presented in italics or in bold. The results showed that young and older adults made equal use of some strategies (e.g., mental imagery, mental repetition), that young adults used sentence generation almost five times more often than older people, and that older adults more often used other strategies (or no strategy) than young people (Figure 4.2).

Cohen and Faulkner (1983) gave young and older participants a test of visuospatial abilities. In this test, participants saw a cartoon figure holding a ball in either its right or left hand. The task was to indicate whether the ball was in the figure's left or right hand. The figure was presented from a variety of angles and orientations (see illustrations in Figure 4.3a). To perform this test of visuospatial abilities, the participants could use the four following strategies: (1) *horizontal rotation*: mentally rotating figures shown with their heads pointing downward both horizontally and vertically; (2) *vertical rotation*: mentally rotating figures shown facing away around their vertical axis to face forward; (4) *own-body reference*: imagining aligning their body to the figure; and (4) *rule strategy*: creating decision rules (e.g., "for inverted front views the left hand is on the left; for inverted back views the left hand is on the right"). The authors not only studied the performance of young and older participants, they also asked participants at the end of the experiment what strategy

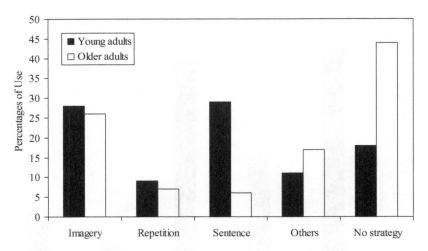

FIGURE 4.2 Percentage use of different source encoding strategies in young and older participants (data from Kuhlmann & Touron, 2012).

they had used. They were thus able to compare the number of participants using each strategy. As can be seen in Figure 4.3b, the percentage of young and older participants who reported using each strategy was very similar.

In their study, Cohen and Faulkner (1983) also asked young and older participants to perform a verbal reasoning task. This task, which is analogous to the one used by Reichle, Carpenter, and Just (2000), described in Chapter 2, was strongly inspired by the research of Clark and Chase (1972). It consisted in presenting a sentence and a figure on a computer screen and asking participants to indicate whether the sentence accurately described the figure (yes/no). In the version of the task used by Cohen and Faulkner (1983), the participants saw sentences such as "X is above O" or "X is not below O" and a drawing that either matched the content of the sentence or did not. The participants had to indicate as quickly as possible whether the sentence fits the drawing. Besides recording participants' performance, the authors asked each participant at the end of the task whether they had used a linguistic strategy (i.e., verbally describing the drawing to themselves and comparing this verbal description to the sentence presented in the trial) or a visual strategy (i.e., creating a mental image of the drawing described by the sentence and comparing it to the drawing). Sixty-six percent of both young and older participants reported using the linguistic strategy, while 34% of each of the two age groups said they had used the visual strategy. Cohen and Faulkner thus found equivalent strategy distributions in young and older participants on both the verbal reasoning task and the test of visuospatial abilities.

Note that in these cases strategy distributions were compared on the basis of the number of participants who reported using each strategy when the experimenter asked at the end of the experiment. It is unclear how accurately these off-line verbal

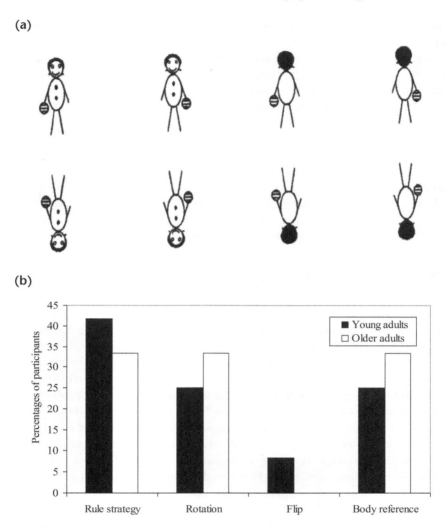

FIGURE 4.3 (a) Test of visuospatial abilities used by Cohen and Faulkner (1986). On each trial, participants saw one of these figures, and had to indicate whether the ball was in the figure's left or right hand. (b) Percentage of young and older participants using each of the visuospatial strategies.

protocols reflect how participants actually performed a task. It could be, for example, that participants who reported using the visual strategy on the verbal reasoning task only used it for a portion of items, possibly even quite a small number of them. This is possible if (as is highly probable) participants use more than one strategy to perform the task, applying different strategies to different items. In other words, besides the fact that it is difficult to draw conclusions on the basis of an absence of difference (between strategy distributions), it could be that the apparently similar strategy distributions found in young and older adults actually mask differences which would be uncovered with the use of appropriate methods. This means assessing the strategy that participants use on each item, and not at the end of the experiment. Note, however, that it is also entirely possible to find strategy differences between young and older adults using off-line verbal protocols (e.g., Hartley & Anderson, 1983). Note also that even probing strategy item by item—as Geary and Lin (1998) did with subtraction problem solving and as Dunlosky and Hertzog (1998, 2001) did with episodic memory—can reveal no differences between the strategy distributions of young and older adults.

In conclusion, some data suggest that the frequency with which young and older adults use each of the strategies to perform some cognitive tasks is similar. As in the case of strategy repertoire, however, this null hypothesis does not stand up to further empirical scrutiny. Another body of experimental data demonstrates differences in how frequently young and older adults make use of different strategies.

Differing strategy distributions in young and older adults

In a study on decision making, Johnson (1990) asked participants to choose which of a set of six cars they would buy, if given the choice. The rows of a matrix displayed on a computer screen represented cars one to six, and its columns corresponded to various characteristics of the cars (fuel economy, handling, riding comfort, maintenance costs, safety, price, styling, and resale value). To make this decision, the participants could ask for these items of information about each car. To obtain information on a given characteristic of a particular car, participants clicked on the box at the intersection of the row for the car and the column for the characteristic, which caused the information to appear (e.g., the price of the second car). Johnson identified two information search strategies: (1) a "compensatory" strategy (i.e., comparing multiple models of cars on multiple characteristics, such as both the price and the riding comfort of a Honda and a Volkswagen); and (2) a "noncompensatory" strategy (i.e., comparing multiple cars on a single characteristic, such as comparing a Honda and a Volkswagen exclusively on price). She observed that the number of participants who used one or the other of these two strategies differed between the young adult and older adult groups (Figure 4.4). Specifically, she found that one young participant and eight older participants used a mixed strategy (both compensatory and noncompensatory); 28 young participants used a compensatory strategy and seven a noncompensatory strategy, while 15 older participants used a compensatory strategy and five a noncompensatory strategy.

Hartley and Anderson (1983) also reported an age difference in strategy distribution on an inductive reasoning task, as measured by the number of participants using each of the available strategies. The authors tested 32 young participants and 32 older participants on a variant of the 20-questions task. In this task, the participants had to determine which of the boxes in a grid the experimenter was thinking of. To do so, the participants had to ask the experimenter yes/no questions (e.g., "Is it in the top row?"). They tested participants

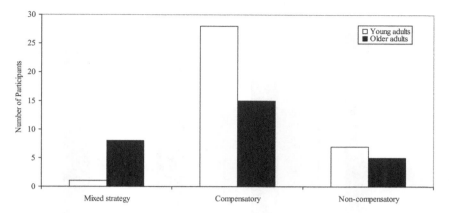

FIGURE 4.4 Number of young and older participants using mixed, compensatory, and noncompensatory strategies in the experiment of Johnson (1990) on decision making. The number of young and older participants using each information search strategy differed.

in four conditions: (1) Condition 1: Participants had to find the target position in an 8 × 8 grid; (2) Condition 2: Participants performed the same task but with a limited time allowance of 60 seconds; (3) Condition 3: Participants had to find the position in a 16 × 16 grid; (4) Condition 4: Participants had to find two positions in an 8 × 8 grid.

The participants were classified according to which of a set of three possible strategies they used: (1) Nonoptimal strategy: The participants asked questions about specific boxes (e.g., "Are you thinking about the box in the top right corner?"); (2) suboptimal strategy: The participant asked questions about a relatively limited set of boxes (e.g., "Is the box you are thinking of in the first column?"); and (c) optimal strategy: The participants asked questions which produced the maximum possible decrease in uncertainty or, equivalently, the maximum information gain (e.g., "Is it in the lower half of the grid?"). The results, which are shown in Figure 4.5, showed that more young adults than older adults used the optimal strategy.

One of the limitations of Hartley and Anderson's (1983) study is that the participants only had one trial in each of the four experimental conditions. A protocol with such a small number of trials cannot capture intra-individual variability (wherein a single individual can use different strategies for different items). In order to genuinely determine whether there are age-related differences in strategy distribution on a task, researchers must: (1) use a task that allows for at least two strategies (which is often the case); (2) test many trials; and (3) assess what strategy each participant used on each trial. The percentage of trials on which each individual in each age group used the different strategies can then be calculated.

Many studies meeting these criteria have been carried out. For example, in a series of studies on numerosity estimation, Gandini and collaborators (Gandini, Lemaire, & Dufau, 2008; see also Gandini, Lemaire, Anton, & Nazarian, 2008;

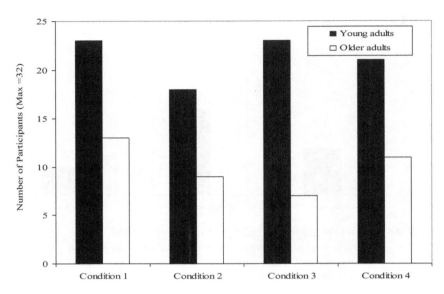

FIGURE 4.5 Number of young and older participants using the optimal strategy in an inductive reasoning task (data from Hartley & Anderson, 1983). The results show that a higher proportion of participants in the young adult group used the optimal strategy in all conditions.

Gandini, Lemaire, & Michel, 2009; Lemaire & Lecacheur, 2007) sought to determine how participants go about approximately assessing the number of dots in a collection that they cannot exactly count. To do so, they gave young and older participants an approximate quantification (also called numerosity estimation) task. They presented collections of dots on a screen for a brief duration (i.e., less than 6 seconds; see Figure 4.6a for an example). The participants were instructed to use whatever strategy they wanted to determine the approximate number of dots contained in each collection. The participants were shown more than 140 collections in each experiment.

Gandini et al. collected verbal protocols (i.e., participants verbally explained how they arrived at an estimate of the number of dots in the collection) for each participant after each item. They discovered that the participants used at least six different strategies (the five shown in Table 4.1, plus the category "Other strategy") to perform this approximate quantification task: Anchoring, estimation, decomposition/recomposition, approximate counting, exact counting, and some "other strategy." Gandini et al. found that the strategy distributions of young and older adults—the proportion of items on which they used each strategy—differed (see Figure 4.6b). Young and older adults were equally likely to use the anchoring strategy, young adults were more likely than older adults to use the estimation and exact counting strategies, and older adults more likely to use the decomposition/recomposition and approximate counting strategies.

(a)

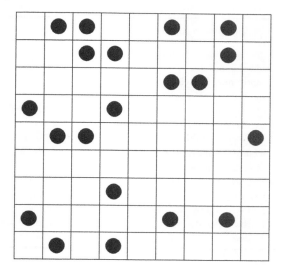

(b)

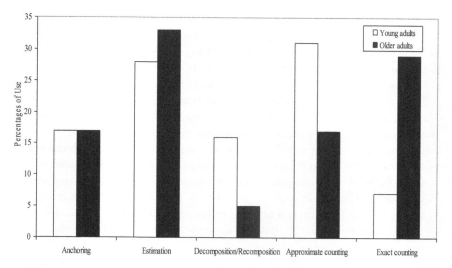

FIGURE 4.6 (a) Example of collections of dots to be approximately quantified, used by Gandini et al. (2009; Gandini, Lemaire, & Dufau, 2008). The participants were free to choose whichever strategy they wanted to determine approximately how many dots were contained in each collection. (b) Percentage use of the different strategies by young and older participants.

TABLE 4.1 List of strategies (and examples of the corresponding verbal protocols) used to approximately quantify collections of dots (from Gandini, Lemaire, & Dufau, 2008)

Strategy	Example of verbal protocol
Anchoring	"I first counted three dots [everywhere], then four dots, added 3 and 4 = 7. Then, I estimated that there remained approximately twice as many dots, so I figured that there are 7 + 14 = 21 dots."
Estimation	"I quickly looked at all the dots, thought it looked like there are about 30 or a little bit more, so I said 32."
Decomposition/ recomposition	"I saw a group of three dots, and I estimated that there were six other similar groups; so I multiplied 7 by 3, and thought there are approximately 21 dots."
Approximate counting	"I first saw two groups of 5 dots, which is 10 dots. Then I saw around 6 dots, which is about 16 dots. Finally, I saw a group of 5 dots. So, there are approximately 21 dots."
Exact counting	"I counted exactly each dot by three: 3, 6, 9, 12; there are 12 dots."

In another numerical task, an exact counting task, Geary and Lin (1998) also observed age-related differences in strategy distributions. Young and older participants saw collections containing between one and seven Xs. The participants could use three strategies: (1) *Subitizing*, wherein they immediately perceived the number of Xs in a collection without counting them (e.g., three Xs were presented and the participant perceived immediately, at a glance, that there were three Xs); (2) *grouping*, consisting in making groups of Xs and adding them together to arrive at the total number (e.g., six Xs were presented and the participant "saw" two groups of three Xs each); and (3) *counting*, consisting in counting the Xs one by one. As Figure 4.7 shows, young and older participants differed in the percentages of trials where they used these different strategies. For example, young adults used the subitizing strategy on 100% of trials with very small collections (one to three Xs), versus 94% for older adults (who used grouping and counting in 2% and 4% of cases respectively). Age-related differences in strategy distributions were still more marked for larger collections (those containing four items or between five and seven items).

Age-related differences in strategy distributions have also been found in the domain of episodic memory. For example, when Bouazzaoui et al. (2010) asked 194 adults between the ages of 21 and 80 years to assess their own use of internal mnemonic strategies (e.g., mental imagery, repetition) and external mnemonic strategies (e.g., making shopping lists, writing down appointments on a calendar), they found that strategy distributions changed with age (Figure 4.8). The older the participants, the more they reported using external strategies to memorize information, and the less they reported using internal strategies (see also Touron, 2006).

Of course, the fact that participants said they had used one or another strategy does not necessarily mean that this is actually what they did (the problem

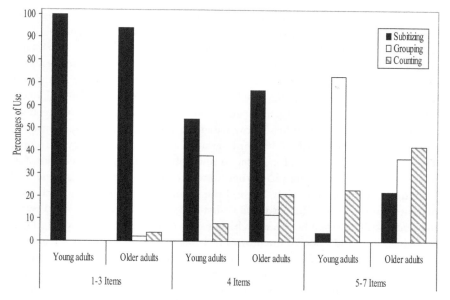

FIGURE 4.7 Mean percentage use of the subitizing (immediate recognition of small quantities), grouping, and counting strategies to quantify the items in collections of between one and seven Xs (data from Geary & Lin, 1998). The results show that the strategy distributions of young and older adults differed for collections of all sizes.

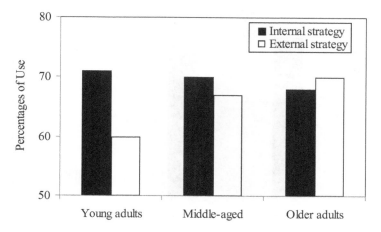

FIGURE 4.8 Percentage use of external and internal strategies reported by young (20–40 years), middle-aged (41–60 years), and older (61–80 years) participants in the study of Bouazzaoui et al. (2010). The older the participants, the more they reported using external strategies and the less they reported using internal strategies.

of validity). This limitation is even more significant when it comes to assessing how *often* individuals use a given strategy—it is unclear that the cognitive system is capable of accurately assessing this. Nevertheless, the findings of Bouazzaoui et al. (2010) converge with data from studies where researchers directly examined the strategies used in episodic memory tasks, without asking participants to estimate how frequently they used each strategy. For example, Bugaiska et al. (2007) tested two groups of participants, young and older adults, on a recognition task using the Remember-Know paradigm (or simply RK paradigm). The participants first saw a list of 36 words, at a pace of one word every 3 seconds. They had to read each word in order to remember it on a subsequent test. Five minutes after this encoding phase, they were shown 72 words one by one. Half were the words from the study list, and the other half were new. For each word presented in this phase, the participants first had to say whether the word was in the study list. They then had to say whether they "remembered" the word (if they thought they could associate memories to it, such as an emotion they felt at the moment of encoding, thoughts, associated images), in which case they gave an R response. They could also give a K response (if they thought they recognized the word without being able to recall any associated memories), or a G response (if they were unsure whether the word was in the study list, but they supposed, or guessed, that it was in the list). As the results presented in Figure 4.9 show, the percentage of R responses decreased significantly with age, whereas the percentages of K and G responses were the same in the two age groups (see also Clarys, Isingrini, & Gana, 2002a, b).

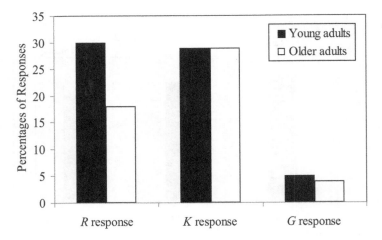

FIGURE 4.9 Percentages of R (recognition with associated memories), K (recognition with no associated memories), and G (guess) responses in young and older participants in the study of Bugaiska et al. (2007). These data show a decrease in R responses in older adults, along with unchanged numbers of K and G responses.

Note that differences in strategy distribution can also be found on tasks where the strategies used can only be determined using indirect methods. For example, Reder, Wible, and Martin (1986) had participants make inferences based on texts they had read. The young and older participants in their experiments were given texts of about 20 lines to read. At the end of each text, the participants were presented with a set of statements. Their task was to indicate whether these statements were present in the text they had just read. Some of these statements were explicitly contained in the text; the others were not. The statements that were not contained in the text were either highly plausible or moderately plausible (see the example text and questions in Table 4.2). To respond to the statements that were actually presented in the text, the participants had to use a retrieval strategy (i.e., retrieve the relevant information from memory). To respond to the statements that were plausible,

TABLE 4.2 Example of a story that young and older participants read in the experiment of Reder et al. (1986), and of highly or moderately plausible statements presented in the recognition task (participants gave a yes/no response indicating whether the statement was contained in the story)

Example story

The heir to a large hamburger chain was in trouble.
He had married a lovely young woman who had seemed to love him.
Now he worried that she had been after his money all along.
He sensed that she was not attracted to him.
Perhaps he consumed too much beer and French fries.
No, he couldn't give up the fries.
Not only were they delicious, he got them for free!
Anyway, real marital strife lay elsewhere.
His wife had never revealed before marriage that she read books.
Sometimes she used words that were many syllables long.
The proud husband decided that she was showing off.
At least, he thought, she stayed at home.
It is not too late, he resolved.
The heir decided to join Weight Watchers.
Twenty-five pounds later, the heir realized his wife did love him after all.
He vowed never to eat another French fry.
He also told his father that he wanted no part of his greasy-food fortune.
The wife of the ex-heir smiled as they went jogging into the sunset.
Tonight she would teach him to read.

Questions

Highly plausible	The heir wanted to lose weight.
	The heir had lost weight.
	The heir got his fries from his father's hamburger chain.
Moderately plausible	The heir had not worried about his wife's motives before marriage.
	The heir wished his wife did not read books.
	Before marriage, his wife hid her superior intellect.

but that were not actually contained in the text, they could either use a retrieval strategy or a plausibility strategy (i.e., assessing whether the information was plausible given the information they had retained). The difference in the rate of correct answers between statements that were contained in the text and those that were not is an indicator of the use of the plausibility strategy. As the mean recognition rates in Figure 4.10 show, in young participants there was no difference between sentences that were present in the text and ones that were absent in the correct recognition rate. Young adults were able to attain correct recognition rates of more than 80% for both types of statements using a retrieval strategy. Older adults, in contrast, tended to use the retrieval strategy to assess the statements that were contained in the text (as shown by their nearly 90% correct recognition rate) and a plausibility strategy to assess statements that were not (as suggested by their near-chance correct recognition rate). It is likely that, because older adults' memory traces of the sentences in the text were too weak and difficult to retrieve, they more often resorted to a plausibility strategy. This strategy difference is interesting since it seems to result more from a limitation in processing resources (and in particular from older adults' weaker memory) than from a truly intentional choice on the participants' part. In other words, it could be that some strategy differences (in strategy repertoire, distribution, or selection) result from cognitive limitations, whereas others reflect deliberate choices linked to factors other than aging-induced cognitive limitations.

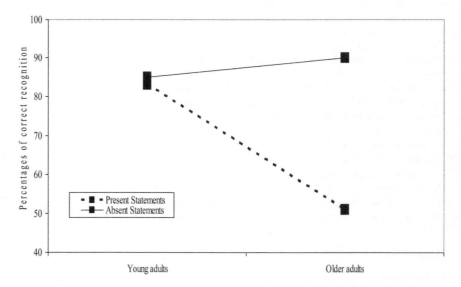

FIGURE 4.10 Percentage of correct recognition of statements either present in or absent from previously read texts in young and older participants (based on Reder et al., 1986). The data show that older participants were more likely to use a plausibility strategy than young participants (who more often used a retrieval strategy).

Modulation of age-related differences in strategy distributions

Age-related differences in strategy distributions are not systematically found. Under some conditions, and for some tasks or items, young and older participants make similar use of available strategies, whereas for other conditions, tasks, and items, young and older adults use different strategies a different proportion of the time.

To take an illustrative example, Robert Siegler and I (Siegler & Lemaire, 1997) asked 48 young participants and 51 older participants to solve multiplication problems. Four types of multiplication problems were tested: $N \times 10$ problems (e.g., 7×10), $NN \times 10$ problems (e.g., 23×10), $N \times NN$ problems (e.g., 4×28), and $NN \times NN$ problems (e.g., 13×48). To obtain the answer to each problem, the participants could choose either to use a mental calculation strategy or to calculate the product using a calculator. We studied the percentage of items in each category that young and older participants solved using a mental calculation strategy. It can easily be seen in Figure 4.11 that on some types of problems there was no difference between young and older adults (i.e., $N \times 10$ and $NN \times NN$ problems), while on the other types of problems there were significant differences between the two age groups (i.e., $NN \times 10$ and $N \times NN$ problems).

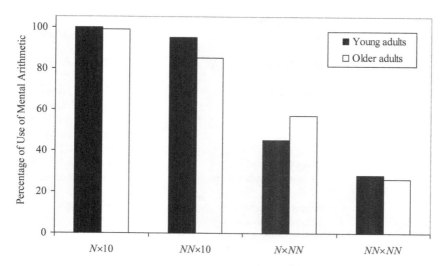

FIGURE 4.11 Percentage use of mental calculation by young and older participants according to problem type (based on Siegler & Lemaire, 1997). The data showed that young and older participants were equally likely to use mental calculation when they solved $N \times 10$ (e.g., 8×10) and $NN \times NN$ (e.g., 23×57) problems, but that they differed when solving $NN \times 10$ (e.g., 43×10) and $N \times NN$ (e.g., 7×38) problems.

Conclusions

In this chapter, we have seen that the strategy distributions of young and older adults sometimes differ such that young and older adults' mean percentages of use of particular strategies for a given task or within a given cognitive domain are often not the same. Such age differences have been observed in many cognitive domains (Table 4.3). In some cases, older people more often use easier strategies (i.e., those with lower cognitive costs and/or which can be executed more quickly), and in others they favor more difficult strategies. The question that immediately arises here is why, in some contexts, older people tend to use more difficult strategies,

TABLE 4.3 A nonexhaustive list of studies showing changes in strategy distribution during aging

Cognitive domain	Type of task used	Study
Acquisition of cognitive abilities	Noun-pair lookup task	Hertzog, Touron, & Hines, 2007; Onyper, Hoyer, & Cerella, 2006, 2008; Rogers, Hertzog, & Fisk, 2000; Touron, 2006; Touron & Hertzog, 2004
	Abstract arithmetic problem solving ("pound arithmetic")	Touron & Hertzog, 2009
	Alphabetic verification	Frank, Touron, & Hertzog, 2013
Visuospatial attention	Mental rotation (LUCY)	Cohen & Faulkner, 1983
Numerical cognition	Numerosity estimation	Gandini, Lemaire, Anton & Nazarian, 2008; Gandini, Lemaire, & Dufau, 2008; Gandini et al., 2009; Lemaire & Lecacheur, 2007
	Exact enumeration	Geary & Lin, 1998
	Complex subtraction problem solving	Geary et al., 1993; Siegler & Lemaire, 1997
	Simple subtraction	Geary & Lin, 1998
Language	Lexical decision (recognition of words/nonwords)	Madden, 1988
	Text-based inference	Reder et al., 1986
Episodic memory	Mnemonic strategy assessment	Bouazzaoui et al., 2010; Clarys et al., 2002a, b
	Source memory task	Kuhlmann & Touron, 2012
	Recognition task (Remember/Know paradigm)	Bugaiska et al., 2007
	Memorization of related word pairs	Dunlosky & Hertzog, 1998

Decision making	Car purchase task	Johnson, 1990
	Diamond choice task	Mata, Schooler, & Rieskamp, 2007
	Yard sale task	Chen & Sun, 2003
	Various choice tasks with economic (e.g., financial) decisions	Li, Baldassi, Johnson, & Weber, 2013
	Iowa Gambling Task	Beitz, Salthouse, & Davis, 2014
Reasoning	Verbal (deductive) reasoning	Cohen & Faulkner, 1983
	Twenty-questions task (inductive reasoning)	Hartley & Anderson, 1983; Hartley, 1986

when they could seemingly use easier ones, as they do in some other conditions. The study of age-related differences in strategy execution, which is the subject of the next chapter, offers interesting insights on this issue.

Work on age-related differences in strategy distributions in different cognitive domains offers important insights on the conditions required to maximize the chances of observing such differences, when they exist. This type of research has shown that studies intended to uncover effects of aging on strategy distributions must: (1) choose a task that allows for the use of multiple strategies, so that strategy variability can emerge and be analyzed; (2) use a large enough number of items to study intra-individual strategy variability; and (3) assess the strategy used, whenever possible, either directly (using immediate or on-line verbal protocols), or else indirectly (on the basis of participants' performance). Such studies can also test the same items (or different items that are strictly matched on a number of characteristics) several times in a single experiment in order to assess whether strategy variability on a given item is found in a particular domain or task. No study on human cognition and cognitive aging has thus far made clear under what conditions strategies vary between presentations of the same items, and what conditions lead participants to use the same strategy each time on repeated items.

The findings discussed in this chapter suggest that, just as it is important to assess strategy repertoire, it is also crucial to determine whether strategy distributions change with aging, in order to understand the origins of age-related differences in cognitive performance. As noted above, young and older adults can use differing strategy repertoires (in which case their strategy distributions will necessarily differ as well). They can also use the same strategy repertoires but differ in how often they use each strategy. For example, if young adults more often use the faster of two strategies and older adults the slower one, then age-related differences in performance will be (at least in large part) due to this difference in strategy distributions. As we will see in the next chapter, performance differences (as well as similarities) sometimes result largely from these differences in distributions. Sometimes, as well, strategy preferences do not contribute to performance differences. In this case, decline in cognitive performance during aging results from other factors, such as decreases in the efficiency of the basic mechanisms that strategies rely on.

5

AGING AND STRATEGY EXECUTION

Chapter outline

Age-related differences in strategy execution when participants choose their own strategies

Age-related differences in strategy execution with controls for selection bias

Interactions between strategy, stimulus features, and situational characteristics during aging

Age-related differences in strategy execution, or differences in measurement sensitivity?

Aging and sequential effects during strategy execution

Conclusions

Even when young and older adults use the same types and number of strategies, and use each strategy the same proportion of the time, their execution of these strategies can differ. Strategy execution is how individuals implement the available strategies, and, in particular, their efficiency in doing so. This can be evaluated through their performance (in terms of speed and accuracy) as well as with recordings of eye movements and brain activations which are correlated with the use of each strategy. In this chapter, we look at whether young and older adults differ in their strategy execution, and if so, to what extent and under what conditions. In the first section, we look at findings on change in strategy execution during aging from studies where participants themselves choose what strategy to use on each item. In the second section, we look at findings from studies that take some biases in strategy selection into account. We examine factors that can influence differences in strategy execution between young and older adults: The characteristics of problems, situations, strategies, and sequences of strategies.

Age-related differences in strategy execution when participants choose their own strategies

Researchers studying participants' performance in various cognitive domains with different strategies have found not only that performance depends on which strategies are used, but also that differences between young and older adults vary depending on which strategies each age group use.

For example, Geary and Wiley (1991) asked 60 young adults and 60 older adults to solve 40 simple addition problems (e.g., 8 + 7). They collected verbal protocols for each problem, asking participants how they had solved it. They found that young participants used three strategies: Verbal counting (e.g., to solve 7 + 2, they counted 7, 8, 9), decomposition (e.g., for 8 + 7, they calculated 8 + 5 + 2 or 8 + 8 − 1) and retrieval (i.e., they directly retrieved the result from long-term memory). Older adults, however, used only two of the three strategies: Decomposition and retrieval. Older participants' performance was slower than that of young adults with each of these two strategies (Figure 5.1). Analyses of overall solution times did not reveal larger time differences between older and young adults with one strategy relative to the other of the two strategies.

Regression analyses predicting retrieval solution times in young and older participants with the size of correct products (the most strongly correlated problem feature

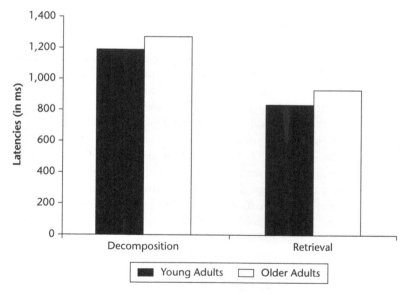

FIGURE 5.1 Mean solution time for simple addition problems (e.g., 8 + 4) in young and older adults for each decomposition and retrieval strategy (based on Geary & Wiley, 1991). These data show that older participants solved the addition problems more slowly than young adults with each of the two strategies.

with solution times) allowed the authors to assess the execution times of the main processes included in the retrieval strategy. They found that young and older adults' respective solution times could be statistically modeled with the following equations:

Young adults: 740 + 3.2 (*Product*)
Older adults: 826 + 3.6 (*Product*)

This means, for example, that the mean solution time (in ms) for 7 + 4 was 830 ms (740 + 3.2(28)) for a young participant and 927 ms (826 + 3.6(28)) for an older participant. The mean solution time for 7 + 8 was 919 ms (740 + 3.2(56)) for a young participant and 1028 ms (826 + 3.6(56)) for an older participant. Each of the two parameters in the equation (the intercept and the slope) characterizes the efficiency of particular processes involved in the strategy. This type of analysis can thus be used to quantify age-related differences in the mean execution times of the processes involved in the retrieval strategy. Geary and Wiley's results revealed that the age-related slowing of the retrieval strategy resulted not from slowed activation of the correct response in long-term memory, but from a slowing of other processes (i.e., encoding the problem, strategy selection, and response). The slope, which was 3.2 for young adults and 3.6 for older adults, reflects the execution time of the process of activation and retrieval of the correct answer from long-term memory. The difference between the coefficients for the two age groups was not statistically significant, suggesting that it took young and older participants the same amount of time to activate the correct answer to a simple addition problem in long-term memory. The intercept in the equation (740 for young adults and 826 for older adults) estimates the duration of the other component processes in the strategy. This difference was statistically significant, indicating that the three processes estimated by this parameter (i.e., encoding of the problem, strategy selection, and response) took an extra 86 ms in older participants. In conclusion, Geary and Wiley discovered that aging is accompanied by a slowing of strategy execution, and that for the retrieval strategy, this slowing occurs in processes other than retrieval itself (see also Allen, Ashcraft, & Weber, 1992; Allen, Smith, Jerge, & Vires-Collins, 1997, Allen et al., 2005 for similar results with multiplication-solving tasks).

Similar results have been reported in episodic memory, where young adults have been found to perform better than older adults regardless of which strategy they use. Dunlosky and Hertzog (2001) asked 32 young adults and 33 older adults to learn a list of word pairs (e.g., *dog–spoon*), each presented for 8 seconds. After encoding each word pair, participants had to report how they had done so. They were invited to choose between a set of possible strategies: Mental imagery, repetition, sentence generation, other strategy, or no strategy. Participants' performance with each strategy was analyzed. As the data presented in Figure 5.2 (for the three most frequently used strategies) show, young participants performed considerably better than older participants regardless of strategy.

Each of these two studies from two different domains (i.e., arithmetic problem solving and episodic memory) offers a typical illustration of cases where the

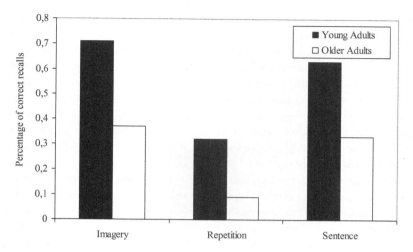

FIGURE 5.2 Proportions of items correctly recalled by young and older participants
with the three main strategies used to encode word pairs (data from
Dunlosky & Hertzog, 2001). These findings show that older participants
performed worse than young participants with each strategy.

performance difference between young and older adults is the same for each of
the strategies used to perform a task. There are many such cases. The problem is
that it is impossible to determine on the basis of these results whether: (1) effects
of aging on performance are the same for all strategies, or (2) these effects are
larger while using some strategies than with other strategies, but in a way that
cannot be detected with the particular protocols used in the study.

One of the limitations of these protocols is what is often called a "selection
effect." Consider the following illustrative example. In a study on the development of mental calculation, Robert Siegler and I (Lemaire & Siegler, 1995)
asked 7-year-old children to solve a set of simple multiplication problems. We
found that these children used a number of strategies, notably repeated addition
(i.e., to solve 3 × 4, they counted 4, 8, 12) and direct retrieval of the answer from
long-term memory. These children, who were tested longitudinally, three times
over the course of a year, took 18.8 seconds per problem using repeated addition
and 3.9 seconds using retrieval in the first session. They took 14.7 seconds and
2.8 seconds respectively in the second session, and 11.8 seconds and 2.9 seconds
in the final session. These results bring out two points. First, retrieval was always
faster than repeated addition. Second, the execution speed of the two strategies changed differently across the three sessions. When we analyzed the types
of problems on which the children used each of the two strategies, we found
that (1) they used retrieval less often than repeated addition, and (2) they used
retrieval more often on problems such as 3 × 4, 4 × 6, and 2 × 3, and repeated
addition more often with problems such as 7 × 8, 9 × 6, and 9 × 7. In other
words, the children tended, particularly in the first session, not only to use the

retrieval strategy less often, but also to use it on problems with small operands, and repeated addition on problems with larger operands. It is possible that the children used retrieval when they were able to execute it quickly and repeated addition the rest of the time. This would increase the differences between the two strategies. It is thus impossible to say whether the performance difference between the two strategies was due to greater difficulty in executing repeated addition than retrieval—for example, because repeated addition involves more numerous and difficult-to-execute processes—or to differences in the types of problems that the children solved with each strategy. Note as well that the type of strategy that the children used to solve each type of problem changed across the different sessions. It is thus impossible to determine whether the difference in how the speed of execution of the two strategies changed over time resulted from a true difference in how much the efficiency of each strategy increased, or from a difference in the type (and frequency) of the problems for which the two strategies were executed. Therefore, in order to compare the relative efficiency of different strategies and how that efficiency changes with age, it is essential to control the types of problems on which each strategy is executed as well as the frequency of use of each strategy, and thus avoid biases due to selection effects.

Age-related differences in strategy execution with controls for selection bias

One way to control for these selection biases is to have participants use all strategies on all problems. This allows us to measure the relative efficiency of the different strategies, as well as how it changes over time, without contamination from differences in the frequencies of strategies or in the types of problems on which they are applied. Strategy differences with aging can thus be compared *ceteris paribus*.

This method, called the choice/no-choice method, was originally proposed by Siegler and Lemaire (1997). It is simple. First, participants are tested under a condition in which they can freely choose to use whichever available strategy they like on each problem. Next, all the participants have to execute the first strategy on all problems (if there is no reason to worry about test–retest effects on the type of problems used) or on a set of matched problems (i.e., ones with exactly the same characteristics), the same for the second strategy, and the third, and so on for all the available strategies. Note that to study strategy execution alone, the choice condition is not needed. The no-choice condition is enough. This method (and variants of it) has been used many times in a variety of domains (see Luwel, Onghena, Torbeyns, Schillemans, & Verschaffel, 2009, for a review).

For example, Gandini, Lemaire, and Dufau (2008) asked young and older participants to estimate the number of dots in a collection briefly presented on a computer screen (Figure 5.3a, b). Half of our participants first had to execute what we called the perceptual estimation strategy (i.e., visually scanning the entire collection and guessing the number of dots, without counting) on 108 collections, and then to use the anchoring strategy (i.e., successively counting collections of three or four dots

(a) **(b)**

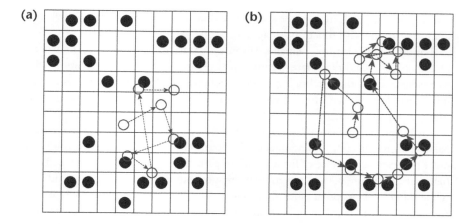

(c)

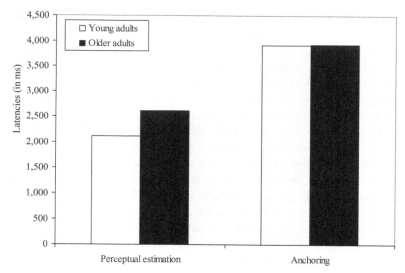

FIGURE 5.3 (a, b) Example of collections of dots to be approximately quantified, used by Gandini et al. (2009; Gandini, Lemaire, & Dufau, 2008). (c) Estimation times (in ms) of young and older participants for each strategy. These data show no age-related difference with the anchoring strategy and an age-related slowing with the perceptual estimation strategy.

and adding together the number of such small collections) on another 108 collections (which were matched on their numerical characteristics—e.g., number of dots—as well as their physical characteristics—e.g., the surface area of the collection as a whole). The other participants used anchoring first and then perceptual estimation. We recorded the participants' performance with each strategy, as well as their eye movements, and, in another study (Gandini, Lemaire, & Michel, 2009), their brain activations with functional magnetic resonance imaging (fMRI).

Gandini et al. (Gandini, Lemaire, Anton, & Nazarian, 2008; Gandini, Lemaire, & Dufau, 2008) found that there was no effect of aging on strategy execution when participants used the anchoring strategy, whereas older participants' estimation times were longer than those of young participants with the perceptual estimation strategy (Figure 5.3c).

Analyzing eye movement (i.e., number and duration of fixations for each participant on each collection), Gandini et al. also found no difference between young and older participants' number of fixations when participants used the anchoring strategy (illustrated in Figure 5.4a, b) nor in their duration, but that both age groups did differ while using the perceptual estimation strategy (see illustration in Figure 5.4a, b). This Age × Strategy interaction in both strategy performance and eye movements has a number of interesting implications. First, it shows that the strategy perspective can allow psychologists who seek to determine which processes are affected during aging and which are spared to do so within a single domain and on a single task. If Gandini and collaborators had merely analyzed participants' performance, they would have found an overall effect of age (with older participants performing more slowly than young participants) on numerosity estimation. They would not, however, have been able to establish that on this task, some processes (those involved in the anchoring strategy) are spared in aging, whereas the efficiency of other processes (involved in the perceptual estimation strategy) decreases during aging. The perceptual estimation strategy involves visuospatial mechanisms, which are known to decline with age (Hale, Myerson, Faust, & Fristoe, 1995; Jenkins, Myerson, Joerding, & Hale, 2000; Lima, Hale, & Myerson, 1991; Vecchi & Cornoldi, 1999); the decrease with age in strategy efficiency is likely in part due to this visuospatial decline. Counting procedures, in contrast, are known to be relatively preserved during aging (e.g., Basak & Verhaeghen, 2003; Geary & Lin, 1998; Sliwinski, 1997; Trick, Enns, & Brodeur, 1996; Watson, Maylor, & Bruce, 2005; Watson, Maylor, & Manson, 2002). These procedures are strongly involved in the anchoring strategy, and doubtless contribute to its preservation with age.

Studies using the choice/no-choice method illustrate the value of controlling for selection biases when assessing age-related differences in strategy performance (execution). Assessing performance in the no-choice condition makes it possible to identify the conditions in which aging negatively affects cognitive performance, and the conditions in which it does not have such deleterious effects. This method also makes it possible to assess the consequences of allowing participants to choose which of several strategies they will use for each item. Figure 5.5 shows the performance of young and older participants in the choice and no-choice conditions on a numerosity estimation task (Gandini et al., 2009) and a currency conversion task (Lemaire & Lecacheur, 2001). As can be clearly seen in the figure, there are cases where the performance difference between young and older participants is decreased when participants can choose their own strategy on each item (e.g., a currency conversion task) and cases where this ability to choose makes no difference (e.g., numerosity estimation).

(a)

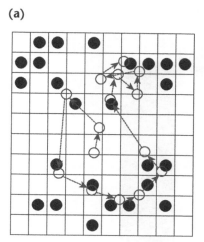

(b)

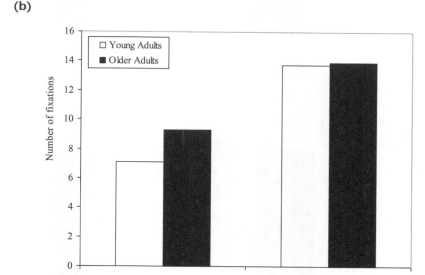

FIGURE 5.4 Illustration of eye movements during the execution of the perceptual estimation (a) and anchoring (b) strategies while estimating the number of dots in a collection of 25. (c) Mean number of fixations with each strategy in young and older participants (based on Gandini, Lemaire, & Dufau, 2008).

It is still too early to tell what task characteristics and conditions lead to the observation of less deleterious effects of aging on cognitive performance in the choice condition, and which do not. One of the hypotheses currently being explored concerns the contribution of strategy selection mechanisms. When these mechanisms carry heavy cognitive costs, it is highly likely that the benefits of being

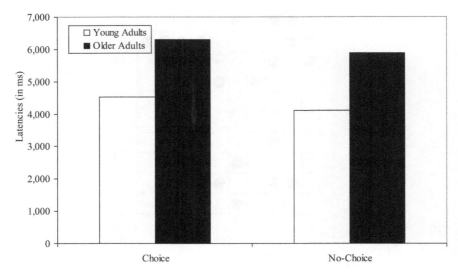

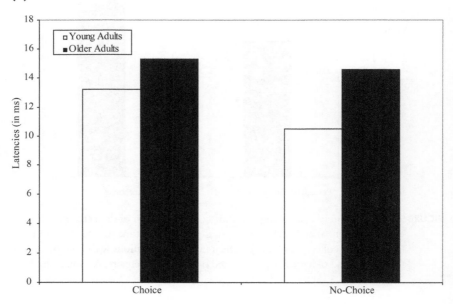

FIGURE 5.5 Age-related performance differences between choice and no-choice conditions (a) on a numerosity estimation task (data from Gandini et al., 2009) and (b) on a currency conversion task (data from Lemaire & Lecacheur, 2001).

able to choose one's strategy on each item will be absorbed (or reduced) by the cognitive costs associated to making the choice. According to this logic, when the cognitive cost of choosing a strategy is low, then age-related performance differences are lower in the choice condition than in the no-choice condition. Put more intuitively, choice may help reduce the effects of aging when the cognitive costs associated to choosing are not too high. Currently, this remains a hypothesis to test.

Consistent with findings on performance and eye movements, neuroimaging data on strategy execution have begun to be collected in a number of cognitive domains. For example, in a study on episodic memory, Kirchhoff, Gordon, and Head (2014) found a correlation between change over time in the quantity of gray matter in the brain (and in particular in the frontal lobes) and the ability to use effective strategies to memorize word lists. The authors administered the California Verbal Learning Test (CVLT-II) to 150 participants between the ages of 18 and 91 years. Participants saw 16 words on a computer screen (four words each from four different categories, such as *drill, paprika, chisel, slacks, plums, tangerines, wrench, grapes, pliers, apricots, nutmeg, jacket, vest, sweater, parsley, chives*), one by one. They then had to recall as many words as possible in whatever order they wanted. The authors also analyzed the quantity of gray matter in the frontal regions of each participant's brain, as well as how they recalled the words. Some individuals, for example, chose to recall all of the words in one category, and then the words in another category, and so on for all four categories. Others recalled the words in some other order. On this basis, the authors classified individuals depending on whether or not they used a semantic clustering strategy (i.e., recalling words by category: Names of fruits first, then names of tools, etc.). They found that the use of semantic clustering was negatively correlated with participants' age. Moreover, it was positively correlated with the volume of gray matter in the participant's frontal and prefrontal brain regions. Statistical analyses showed that the decrease in gray-matter volume with age mediated the decrease in the use of the semantic clustering strategy in older adults. Moreover, the use of the serial recall strategy (i.e., recalling words in order of their presentation) was also negatively correlated with age, although the use of this strategy was not correlated with gray-matter volume in prefrontal regions. This last result shows that the decrease in the quantity of gray matter with age does not mediate all variance in performance, and thus that the observed mediation of age effects on strategy selection by gray-matter volume is not simply a consequence of such a general effect.

The study of Kirchhoff, Gordon, and Head (2014) offers evidence of a brain basis for strategy variations with age. More generally, their results are consistent with the hypothesis that neuroanatomical changes, which have long been known to lead to changes in cognitive performance (e.g., Cabeza, Nyberg, & Park, 2005; Raz, 2000), may also produce other changes in cognitive function, notably at the level of the strategies individuals use to perform a cognitive task. As interesting as this conclusion is, two observations must be made about the results of the study. First, the correlations that were found to be significant were not large, particularly given the large sample size (below $r = 0.25$). Next, and more critically, the strategies used were not assessed independently of performance on the recall task. Correct word recall was used to determine what strategies the participants had used. But when using this type of analysis, it is important to assess performance and strategy independently, if at all possible, and (again, if possible) to do so for each item separately.

Gandini, Lemaire, Anton, and Nazarian (2008) did just this in a neuroimaging study, using fMRI. We studied age-related differences in brain activations while participants used the perceptual estimation strategy or the anchoring strategy to estimate the number of dots in collections like those seen above. While using the perceptual estimation strategy, older participants showed higher levels of brain activation than young participants in middle temporal gyrus, left dorsolateral prefrontal cortex, left supramarginal gyrus, and left precuneus. While using the anchoring strategy, right superior frontal gyrus, left lower parietal lobe, right cuneus, and right superior temporal gyrus were markedly more highly activated in older participants than in young participants. Note that these brain activations were obtained in a no-choice condition, and thus while controlling not only for the strategy used on each item, but also for the frequency of use of each strategy.

One of the valuable aspects of these studies by Gandini and collaborators is the demonstration that the effects of aging on cognitive performance (as well as on brain activations) are modulated by the type of strategy that participants are using. In fact, they are also modulated by the type of problem solved and, more generally, by the type of information that is processed in the task. An Age × Strategy × Item interaction has been observed in a number of studies. For example, in a study on age-related differences in the solution of addition problems with two three-digit numbers (e.g., 246 + 753), Green, Lemaire, and Dufau (2007) found that the modulation of aging effects by the strategy used depended on the type of problems that participants were solving. We compared 24 young participants and 24 older participants using the "hundred strategy" and the "unit strategy" in this addition problem. The unit strategy consists in adding the unit digits, then the decades, then the hundreds (e.g., to solve 246 + 753, first adding 6 + 3 = 9, then 4 + 5 = 9, then 2 + 7 = 9, yielding 999). The hundred strategy consists in performing the same set of operations, but in the reverse order (e.g., first 2 + 7 = 9, then 4 + 5 = 9, and finally 6 + 3 = 9, yielding 999). The problems included one or two carries (e.g., 246 + 738, 276 + 758), or none (e.g., 246 + 753). We recorded strategy performance (Figure 5.6a) and eye movements (Figure 5.6b).

In terms of strategy performance, the data showed that the dependence of the age-related performance difference on the strategy used differed between problems involving at least one carry and problems without a carry. For example, when the participants were solving no-carry problems, the differences between young and older participants' error rates (i.e., older adults' error rate − young adults' error rate) with the hundred strategy and the unit strategy were 1.6% and 2.6%, respectively. When they were solving problems with one or two carries, the corresponding differences between young and older adults were 10.9% and 6.3%. These data show that the effects of aging are interactively modulated by the type of strategy used and the type of problem solved.

(a)

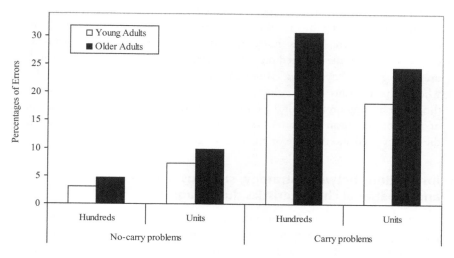

(b)

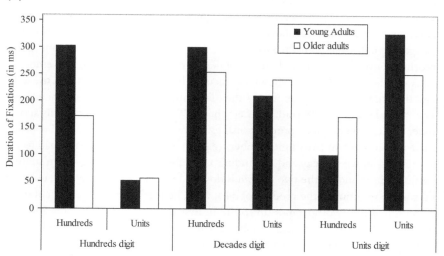

FIGURE 5.6 (a) Mean percentages of errors committed by young and older participants while executing the hundred strategy or the unit strategy during the addition of two three–digit numbers with or without a carry (e.g., 126 + 358, 123 + 456); (b) mean duration of gaze fixations during the first second following the visual onset of the problem, by strategy (data from Green et al., 2007).

The same Age × Strategy × Problem interaction was found with eye movements, as Figure 5.6b shows. The difference between the mean fixation durations of young and older adults during the first second of strategy execution was −132 ms (i.e., older adults' fixations were 132 ms shorter than those of young adults), and 4 ms when they were fixating the hundred digit while executing the hundred strategy and the unit strategy, respectively. The corresponding differences were −46 ms and 30 ms when the participants were fixating on the decade digit, and 70 ms and −75 ms when they were fixating on the unit digit. In other words, as for the error rate, the effects of aging on the mean duration of eye fixations were interactively affected by both the strategy used and the type of problem solved.

Interactions between strategy, stimulus features, and situational characteristics during aging

The data presented above show that the effects of aging are influenced by the strategies that participants use and the type of problems they have to solve. The final factor that modulates the effects of aging when participants are executing different strategies is the characteristics of the situation. In both daily life and in the laboratory, young and older adults can perform a range of cognitive tasks using different strategies to solve different types of problems, in situations which can vary along a number of dimensions, such as having to respond either very quickly or else under no particular speed constraints. Other characteristics of the situation can include, for example, performing a cognitive task while alone in a room or in the company of a peer or a group, in the morning or the afternoon, and under conditions of stress, fatigue, or strong emotion.

A number of studies have shown interactions between participants' age, the strategy they use, the types of problems they face, and such situational characteristics. For example, Lemaire, Arnaud, and Lecacheur (2004) asked 96 young adults and 96 older adults to perform a computational estimation task, working out the approximate product of two two-digit numbers (e.g., 34 × 68). The participants had to use a rounding-down strategy and a rounding-up strategy. The rounding-down strategy consisted in rounding the two operands down to the nearest decade (e.g., use 30 × 60 = 1800 to estimate the product of 34 × 68). The rounding-up strategy consisted in rounding the two operands up to the nearest decade (e.g., 40 × 70 = 2800 for 34 × 68). The participants had to solve so-called *rounding-down problems*, where the rounding-down strategy provided a more accurate estimate (e.g., 36 × 62), and so-called rounding-up problems, where the rounding-up strategy yields a more accurate result (e.g., 27 × 64). The participants had to use the rounding-down strategy for half of problems and the rounding-up strategy for the other half. Finally, the participants were tested in a condition where the instructions emphasized accuracy (i.e., the participants were told they should provide estimates that were as close as possible to the exact product) and in a condition where the experimenter did not emphasize the accuracy of the estimated product. We looked at how the participants' performance varied with their age, the type of strategy they were using, the problem they were solving, and the situation.

As Figure 5.7 shows, young and older participants' solution times with each strategy varied with accuracy pressure and the type of problem. While young participants were faster than older participants with both strategies and in both accuracy-emphasis situations (except with the rounding-up strategy), accuracy pressure modulated the two groups' strategy execution differently. While both groups tended to slow down when the instructions placed a greater emphasis on accuracy, older adults slowed down less than younger adults specifically when they were using the more difficult strategy on rounding-down problems, the rounding-up strategy (this is what led them to be more rapid, but less accurate). In other words, older adults were less efficient than young adults at calibrating their strategy execution to the different task constraints (i.e., the type of problem, strategy, and situation). Most likely, due to a decrease in cognitive resources with aging, older adults had less cognitive resources to allocate to calibration operations.

Such modulations of the relationship between aging and strategy type by task and/or stimulus type have been observed in other cognitive domains; they are not specific to numerical cognition. It may even be a general characteristic of human cognition. For example, in a study on episodic memory, Dirkx and Craik (1992; see also Eysenck, 1974; Taconnat & Isingrini, 2004; see the review of Craik, 2002) asked 18 young adults and 18 older adults to learn lists of words for later recall. The participants were tested in three conditions. They were instructed to use a repetition strategy (i.e., repeating each word in the list aloud) in the first condition, the generation of mental images (i.e., creating a mental image with each word and linking the images to each other) in the second condition, and a sentence generation strategy

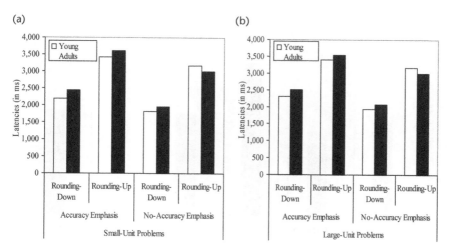

FIGURE 5.7 Computational estimation times of young participants when tested with and without accuracy pressure, by strategy used and type of problem estimated (data from Lemaire et al., 2004). These data show that strategy execution is jointly influenced by the type of strategy used, the type of problem solved, and the constraints of the situation in which the cognitive activity takes place.

(i.e., constructing a sentence or a story with the words in the list) in the last condition. They had to use a different strategy with each of the three lists of 16 words. Each list included both concrete words (e.g., *table*) and abstract words (e.g., *justice*).

The data showed that young and older adults' performance with the different strategies varied depending on whether they were used to encode abstract or concrete nouns. Participants recalled more concrete words than abstract words in all conditions (Figure 5.8). But the data on the effect of aging (i.e., the difference between young and older participants) on the number of correctly recalled words showed that the difference between young and older adults was greater for abstract words than for concrete words (differences of 2.3 and 0.9 for abstract and concrete words, respectively) with the repetition strategy, whereas the age effect was greater for concrete words than for abstract words with the sentence construction (5.3 vs. 3.7) and mental imagery (6.0 vs. 3.3) strategies.

Interactions between the characteristics of situations, items, and strategies are not always found. For example, in a study on encoding strategies, Froger, Taconnat, Landré, Beigneux, and Isingrini (2009) showed that, as in arithmetic problem solving, in episodic memory, the effects of aging on memory capacity are modulated by the type of strategy used, the type of item to be memorized, and the type of task to be performed. The authors asked young and older participants to learn lists of 20 words, each presented for 3 seconds. The participants were tested in a deep encoding strategy condition and a shallow encoding strategy condition. In the first case, they were instructed to encode each word deeply, saying whether the word designates a concrete or an abstract entity. In the shallow encoding strategy, the participant had to determine whether the first or last letter of each word was

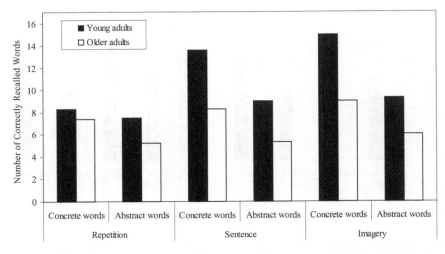

FIGURE 5.8 Number of concrete and abstract words correctly recalled by young and older participants as a function of strategy used in the study of Dirkx and Craik (1992). The data show that the effects of aging were modulated differently by strategy type and item type depending on the recall task.

an "e." The participants' memory was then probed using a free-recall test and a recognition test. On the free-recall test, they were asked to recall as many of the words in the list as they could. On the recognition task, they were shown 40 words, half of which were the words in the study list. The participants had to indicate whether each word had been in the study list or not.

Their mean percentages of correct recognition and recall in different conditions are shown in Figure 5.9. They reveal at least two interesting results. First of all, the performance difference between young and older adults was greater in the deep encoding condition (young and older adults correctly recalled or recognized 64% and 54% of words, respectively) than in the shallow encoding condition (wherein young and older adults correctly recalled or recognized 19% and 15% of words, respectively). Moreover, the difference between young and older adults' performance was modulated both by the strategy used and by the recall task. For example, older adults performed better than young adults on the recognition task after a shallow encoding, but worse in all other conditions (see also Fay, Isingrini, & Clarys, 2005, for similar data from more implicit episodic memory tasks, such as word-fragment and word-stem completion tasks).

In a study on decision making, Mata, Wilke, and Czienskowski (2009) asked 45 young participants and 45 older participants to perform the so-called fishing task (a laboratory analogue of various search tasks: For information, jobs, housing, partners, food, etc.). In this task, the participants were shown a pond and a fisherman on a computer screen. They could "catch" the fish, which are partly camouflaged by a visual background, by tapping on the corresponding location on the screen. The participants could see how many fish they had caught in a given pond, but they did not know how many fish could be caught there. Their objective was to catch as many

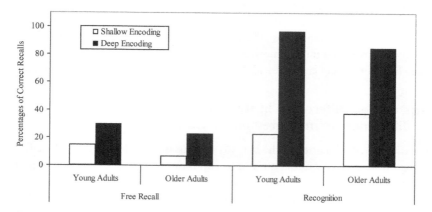

FIGURE 5.9 Young and older participants' percentages of correct recall/recognition on free recall and recognition tasks, after using deep or shallow encoding strategies (data from Froger et al., 2009). These data show that differences between young and older adults' performance were modulated by the type of strategy they used when encoding items.

fish as possible in 40 minutes. Crucially, the authors varied the travel time between ponds. When the participants clicked on the "change ponds" button, another pond appeared either after a relatively short interval (15 seconds) or a relatively long one (30 seconds). Moreover, the instructions given to participants indicated how to use the optimal strategy. More precisely, the following instructions were given:

> Please apply the following strategy for switching ponds: Determine an initial time span with which you want to stay at the pond even if no fish appears and let this time elapse. If no fish appears within that time span, then switch immediately to the next pond. However, if you see a fish within that time span, prolong the time span with which you originally planned on staying at the pond (by adding a little time to the remaining staying time). Repeat this step each time a fish appears. Only leave the pond when no further fish appear within this time span.

In addition to the number of fish participants caught (older adults caught fewer than young adults), the authors analyzed the time that participants spent at each pond. They also looked at the relationship between the optimal amount of time that participants should have spent at each pond (to maximize the number of fish caught) and the time they actually spent. This allowed them not only to determine whether the time participants spent at each pond deviated from the optimum, but to check whether it varied depending on travel time between ponds. Both young and older participants deviated from the optimal time. Young adults took 73 seconds and 91 seconds (vs. optimal times of 33 seconds and 45 seconds) in the short and long travel time conditions, respectively. The corresponding figures for older adults were 88 seconds and 113 seconds. The participants were thus quite far from the optimal times, although older participants were more so than young ones. More interestingly, the two groups showed comparable abilities to adjust their execution time to the travel time between ponds. The increase in the time each group spent at a given pond with increased travel time was similar. In other words, in this case the difference between young and older adults was not modulated by the task parameters.

Age-related differences in strategy execution, or differences in measurement sensitivity?

Clearly, the data discussed in the last two sections suggest that, to study the effects of aging on strategy execution, it is important to carefully control the type of strategy that participants use. It seems, moreover, that the choice of how to measure strategy execution is also important. Certain behavioral measures (such as reaction times and percentage of errors) can prove insufficiently sensitive. In such cases, other more sensitive measures must be used. Osorio, Fay, Pouthas, and Ballesteros (2010; see also Osorio, Ballesteros, Fay, & Pouthas, 2009) did just that in a study on age-related differences in implicit memory (a memory system that works without intentional retrieval of the target information).

Osorio and collaborators explicitly asked their participants to memorize the words in a list using either a shallow encoding (i.e., a so-called lexical strategy consisting in counting the number of syllables in each word) or a deep encoding (i.e., a so-called semantic strategy consisting in indicating whether the meaning of the word was pleasant, unpleasant, or neutral). The participants then saw three-letter word stems, which they had to complete with the first suitable word that came to mind. Certain stems fit with city names that had been in the study lists; others were new. All of the stems had been carefully chosen to be completable with both the name of a city or with another type of noun.

The authors studied the percentages of stems completed with words that had been present in the previously presented list) and with other words (Figure 5.10). The data showed that the participants tended to complete the stems with words they had seen recently (i.e., which were in the study list) more often than with other words: This is known as a priming effect. Very interestingly, priming effects were larger in older adults than in young adults, notably because older adults showed a greater tendency to complete the roots with words that they had previously seen. Moreover, the priming effect was greater in the deep (semantic) encoding condition than in the shallow (lexical) encoding condition, in both young and older participants. In other words, the strategy used does not seem to have changed either the effect of age on the number of completed stems or the age-related difference in priming effects. This suggests that, other than older adults' stronger tendency to complete stems with words they had previously seen,

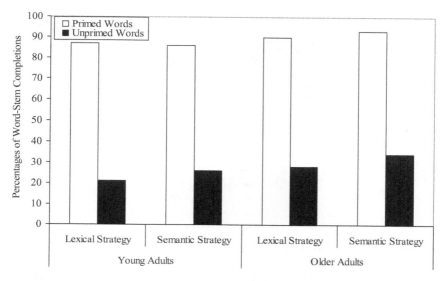

FIGURE 5.10 Implicit memory in young and older participants when using a lexical strategy or a semantic strategy to encode words (data from Osorio et al., 2010). The data show similar priming effects in young and older participants with each of the two strategies.

at the behavioral level, there was no difference in strategy execution between young and older participants.

Osorio et al. also collected evoked potentials data (Figure 5.11). Priming effects were also found in evoked potentials (i.e., differences in evoked potentials between primed and unprimed items, with a greater positivity for the former than for the latter). These effects were similar with the lexical and semantic strategies. However, they were differently localized in young and older adults. In young participants, priming effects were localized in posterior areas (specifically, left parieto-occipital areas), while in older participants they were localized in both posterior areas (as in young participants) and in anterior (fronto-central) areas. In other words, priming

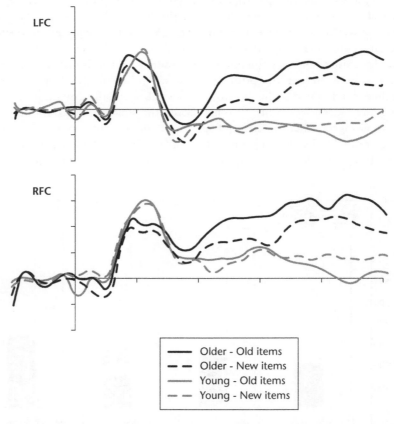

FIGURE 5.11 Evoked potentials associated to young and older adults' execution of the lexical strategy while completing word stems either corresponding to primed words or not, in the experiment of Osorio et al. (2010). LFC, left fronto-central electrodes; RFC, right fronto-central electrodes. The data show priming effects (old–new) localized in the left hemisphere in young participants and bilaterally (i.e., in both right and left hemispheres) in older participants.

effects appeared in parieto-occipital areas in both groups and in frontal areas only in the older group. It is as if the older adults had recruited additional (frontal) brain areas to execute the two encoding strategies. This pattern of recruitment of additional brain areas has often been observed in the cognitive neuroscience of aging. It is the characteristic feature of what Davis, Dennis, Daselaar, Fleck, and Cabeza (2008) called the Posterior–Anterior Shift with Aging (PASA) model. It is often interpreted as a result of the implementation of neural compensation mechanisms. The increased activation of frontal areas in older adults is often accompanied by decreased activation in occipito-parietal areas. According to this interpretation, it is as if an age-related deficit in posterior activation were compensated by greater activation in anterior areas.

Note that the strategy perspective taken in this book suggests two possible hypotheses at the functional level. First, young and older adults may use different strategies. It could be that young adults use strategies which call more on posterior areas and older adults use strategies which draw more on anterior areas. A second possible hypothesis is that young and older adults use the same strategies, but older people need to make greater use of frontally localized brain resources (which suggests that they might rely on additional mechanisms, such as executive functions, which are known to be based in frontal and prefrontal cortex). And while the young and older groups were both instructed to use a lexical strategy and a semantic strategy, there is no guarantee that the two groups executed these strategies in the same way. For example, the semantic strategy (saying whether the word's meaning is pleasant, unpleasant, or neutral) can be executed in a number of different ways (including in cases where both groups indicate that an item is "pleasant," since the levels of evocation and pleasantness can differ between the groups). It is also possible to execute the lexical strategy (i.e., counting the number of syllables in each word) in different ways (e.g., counting syllables while reading the word and forming a mental image of it is not the same strategy as counting the syllables without reading the word and/or creating a mental image). It is important, then, to control as many factors as possible when comparing strategy execution in young and older adults, doing as much as possible to ensure that the two groups execute the same strategies in exactly the same way.

Aging and sequential effects during strategy execution

The results of a number of recent studies suggest that the execution of a strategy on a given item is influenced by the strategy used on the previous item. The results also show that some of these sequential effects are amplified with aging, while others remain stable. The effects that are amplified during aging concern strategy switch costs and sequential modulations of poorer-strategy effects; the effects that are relatively stable are strategy sequential difficulty effects.

Following Lemaire and Lecacheur's (2010) observation of strategy switch costs, Ardiale, Hodzik, and Lemaire (2012) asked 40 young adults and 40 older adults to solve 96 addition problems with two two-digit numbers (e.g., 42 + 84). On each problem, the participants saw an indicator of what strategy they had to execute. In one condition, the so-called two-strategy condition, the participants were asked to execute either the unit strategy or the decade strategy. The unit strategy consisted of adding together first the unit digits, and then the decades (i.e., adding 2 + 4 = 6, then 80 + 40 = 120, and finally 120 + 6 = 126). The decade strategy consisted of adding together first the decades, and then the units (i.e., adding 40 + 80 = 120, and then 4 + 2 = 6, and finally 120 + 6 = 126). In the second condition, the three-strategy condition, the participants had to use these two strategies as well as the so-called borrowing strategy. This strategy consisted of borrowing the unit digit from one of the two operands, adding it to the other operand, and then adding the first operand without its units (e.g., adding 42 + 4 = 46, and then 46 + 80 = 126). In each condition, the participants had to either repeat the same strategy on two successive problems (repeated-strategy trials) or switch strategies between problems (unrepeated-strategy trials). The authors compared strategy execution times on these two types of trials.

As the data in Figure 5.12 show, the performance of both young and older participants was faster when repeating the strategy from the previous trial than following a strategy switch. In the two-strategy condition, young and older participants showed similar strategy switch costs (mean latency on unrepeated-strategy trials − mean latency on repeated-strategy trials). In the three-strategy condition, in contrast, the strategy switch costs were higher in older participants (mean costs: 849 ms) than in young participants (mean costs: 405 ms). In keeping with the explanations in

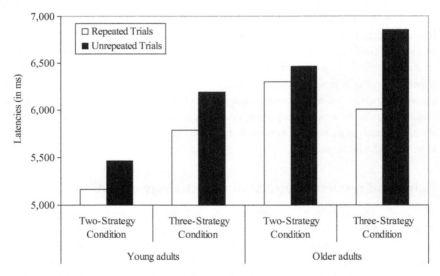

FIGURE 5.12 Latencies on repeated-strategy and unrepeated-strategy trials in young and older adults (data from Ardiale et al., 2012). These data show that strategy switch costs (i.e., latency on unrepeated-strategy trials − latency on repeated-strategy trials) only increased with age in the condition where participants had to manage three strategies.

the general literature on cognitive control and task-switch costs (see Meiran, 2010; Vandierendonck, Liefooghe, & Verbruggen, 2010, for reviews), strategy switch costs can be explained by the involvement of executive control (inhibiting the strategy executed on the previous trial and activating the strategy to be executed on the current trial) on unrepeated-strategy trials. On this interpretation, these control mechanisms are less efficient in older people, but this efficiency disadvantage is only observed in the condition where the participants have to manage a greater number of strategies.

Recently, Lemaire and Hinault (2014) observed another sequential effect that varies during aging. This effect is called sometimes the sequential strategy-poorer effect, sometimes strategy sequential interference effect, or the strategy sequential congruency effect. We gave 67 young participants and 67 older participants a computational estimation task. Their task was to estimate the product of two two-digit numbers using the indicated strategy on each trial. This could be a mixed rounding-down strategy (i.e., rounding the first operand down to the nearest decade and the second up to the nearest decade, such as computing 40 × 60 to estimate 42 × 57) or a mixed rounding-up strategy (i.e., rounding the first operand up to the nearest decade and the second operand down to the nearest decade, such as computing 50 × 50 to estimate 47 × 54). The participants had to execute the best of the two available strategies on some problems (e.g., a mixed rounding-down strategy for 42 × 37) and the poorer of the two on other problems (e.g., mixed rounding-up to estimate 42 × 37). Earlier findings had highlighted a so-called poorer-strategy effect, showing that participants' performance is slower when they are asked to execute a poorer strategy to solve a problem than when they are asked to execute a better strategy (e.g., Lemaire et al., 2004). To investigate whether these poorer-strategy effects are modulated by whether the previous problem had been solved using either a better strategy or a poorer strategy, we tested four experimental conditions. In the different conditions, both the previous and the current problems were to be solved by either the better or the poorer strategy. In the better-better condition, both the previous and the current problems had to be solved with the better strategy; in the better-poorer condition, the previous problem was to be solved with the better strategy and the current problem with the poorer strategy; in the poorer-better condition it was the opposite (poorer strategy on the previous problem, better strategy on the current problem); and in the poorer-poorer condition the poorer strategy was used on both the previous and current problems. The estimation times of young and older participants are shown in Figure 5.13.

In young adults, the poorer-strategy effects were only significant on problems that followed problems that had been solved using the better strategy (poorer-strategy effects: 750 ms), and not when they followed problems on which the poorer strategy had been used (a nonsignificant difference of 136 ms was found in this case). In older adults, in contrast, there were significant poorer-strategy effects following problems solved with both the better (590 ms) and the poorer strategy (685 ms). In other words, only young participants showed a sequential modulation of poorer-strategy effects.

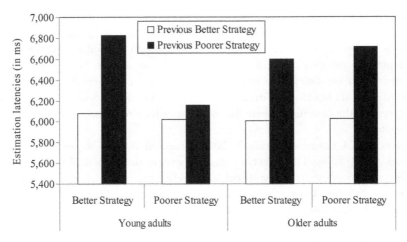

FIGURE 5.13 Estimation times of young and older participants on the current problems according to whether the strategy used on the current and previous problems was the better or poorer strategy (data from Lemaire & Hinault, 2014).

We explained the sequential modulations of poorer-strategy effects by postulating that control mechanisms worked more efficiently in the conditions where the previous problems had been solved using the poorer strategy. That is, when participants had to execute the poorer strategy, they had to inhibit the execution of the better strategy, which was activated more quickly and spontaneously, in order to activate and focus their attention on the required poorer strategy. This prepared them for the possibility that the poorer strategy could be required on the following problem as well. They thus prepared themselves for the possibility of once again avoiding the better strategy. This attentional preparation likely helped them to allocate more attentional resources to the cue which indicated which strategy they had to use on each problem. The execution of the better strategy, in contrast, likely did not lead the participants to expect to have to use the poorer strategy on the following problem. They thus did not prepare themselves to inhibit the better strategy when encoding the problem and/or to pay more attention to the cue. Their attentional resources, which were mainly allocated to encoding the operands, thus led them to more strongly activate the better strategy, which they then had to inhibit in order to use the indicated (poorer) strategy. Older people, however, did not prepare themselves more to use the poorer strategy after a problem where they used it than after one where they had used the better strategy. An age-related decrease in available processing resources likely stopped them from anticipating and attentionally preparing for the following trial in this way.

Further analyses allowed us to uncover that in reality there were two subgroups of older participants: One that showed no sequential modulation of the difference between the better and poorer strategies, and another that showed a difference similar to the one seen in young participants. The data thus suggested that there are large individual differences between older adults in sequential effects. Complementary measures revealed that one of the main differences between the two groups of older participants was that the group whose pattern of results resembled that of younger people showed substantially more efficient executive function than the group which showed no sequential modulation of the strategy interference effect.

In another study, Hinault, Lemaire and Phillips (2016; see also Hinault, Dufau, & Lemaire, 2014) sought to shed further light on the mechanisms involved in the sequential modulations of poorer-strategy effects using evoked potentials. We also sought to determine whether older adults who are as capable of sequentially modulating their management of poorer-strategy effects as young adults succeed in doing so by recruiting additional mechanisms. To do this, we performed a new study wherein we first matched our two groups (one of young participants and one of older participants) at the behavioral level on the basis of this type of sequential modulation. That is, we ensured that, in terms of latencies, the participants in the two age groups showed comparable sequential modulations of poorer-strategy effects. We then studied the electrophysiological signatures of sequential modulations of poorer-strategy effects. Examining the difference in evoked potentials between trials where participants used the poorer strategy and trials where they used the better strategy, we determined whether this difference varied depending on which of the two strategies had been used in the preceding problem. In both young and older participants, the data revealed two electrophysiolagial markers of sequential modulations of the strategy interference effect, one early and one late (Figure 5.14).

The electrophysiological data suggested that two types of executive control mechanisms were recruited to modulate poorer-strategy effects from one trial to the next. Early mechanisms may be active while encoding the problem, and later mechanisms while executing the selected strategy. When they encoded the problem, participants activated the better strategy more or less automatically. For example, on a problem such as 41×54, they activated the rounding-down strategy. But if the problem was presented along with the cue indicating that the poorer strategy (here, the rounding-up strategy) should be used, they had to inhibit the better strategy that was activated at the time of (or just after) the encoding of the operands in order to activate the relevant procedures. Subsequently, as they executed these procedures, they had to continue to inhibit the better strategy. After a problem where they were required to execute the poorer strategy, the participants likely tried to focus more on the cue to the required strategy on the following problem, avoiding focusing their attention exclusively on the characteristics of the operands (like the unit digits), which would quickly activate the better strategy. This allowed them to control the activation of the better strategy in order to activate the required poorer strategy. These control mechanisms were thus activated early, simultaneously with, or just after the encoding of the operands. While then executing the required strategy, participants had to remain vigilant in order not to give in to the temptation to execute the better strategy, which meant inhibiting that strategy. Both types of mechanisms

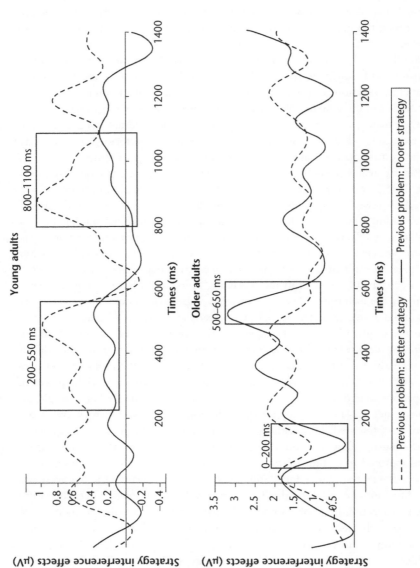

FIGURE 5.14 Difference in evoked potentials during the execution of the poorer and better strategies on a problem following the execution of either the better or the poorer strategy on the previous problem (data from Hinault et al., 2014). The data show that both young and older participants used early and late executive control mechanisms, although they were activated earlier in the older group than in the young group.

were facilitated when the problem followed the execution of the poorer strategy, which led the participant to prepare to manage strategy interference.

Another interesting aspect of the evoked potentials observed by Hinault et al. is that activation of these two types of control mechanisms occurred earlier in older participants than in young participants. The traces of the early mechanisms appeared between 0 and 200 ms after the appearance of the problem in older participants and between 200 and 550 ms in young participants, while the later mechanisms were active between 500 and 650 ms after problem onset in older participants and between 800 and 1100 ms in young participants. In other words, these data revealed an age-related difference in the timecourse of control mechanisms. Hinault et al. carefully selected their older participants, matching them to their young adult group at the behavioral level on the sequential modulations of poorer-strategy effects. It could thus be that this group of older adults was a very particular group of adults with extremely efficient cognitive functions, who had experienced what is called successful aging. In this group of select older adults, faster activation of cognitive control mechanisms allowed them to sequentially modulate their management of strategy interference at the behavioral level as efficiently as the young participants.

In other words, older adults seem to have differed from young adults in showing greater levels of some sequential effects, such as strategy switch costs and the inter-trial modulations of poorer-strategy effects. It also seems that there are large individual differences among older adults in sequential effects. In particular, in older people whose executive control mechanisms are as efficient as those of young adults, sequential effects similar to those observed in young adults are also found. Note, finally, that age-related differences are not observed in all sequential effects on strategy execution.

Uittenhove and Lemaire (2012), for example, reported a sequential effect that does not seem to increase with age: The strategy sequential difficulty effect. We tested 25 young adults and 25 older adults, asking them to perform a computational estimation task (i.e., finding the approximate sum of two two-digit numbers). On each problem, participants had to execute a strategy that was indicated by a cue. This could be a rounding-down strategy (i.e., rounding the two operands down to the nearest decade, such as computing 30 + 50 to estimate 34 + 57), a rounding-up strategy (i.e., rounding the two operands up to the nearest decade, such as computing 40 + 60 to estimate 34 + 57), or a mixed-rounding strategy (i.e., rounding the first operand down to the nearest decade and the second operand up to the nearest decade, such as computing 30 + 60 to estimate 34 + 57). Each trial included two successive problems. The participants' performance with the mixed-rounding strategy on the second problem in a trial differed depending on which strategy had been used in the first problem in the trial (Figure 5.15). The participants' execution was slower when the mixed-rounding strategy followed the rounding-up strategy (which was the most difficult) than after the rounding-down strategy (the easiest) or the mixed-rounding strategy (which in this case was repeated). We labeled this phenomenon the strategy sequential difficulty effect. This effect was interpreted as a result of the need to use more cognitive resources to execute the more difficult

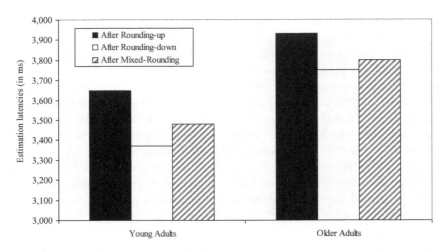

FIGURE 5.15 Young and older participants' execution time with the mixed-rounding strategy when estimating the sum of two numbers according to the strategy used on the previous problem (data from Uittenhove & Lemaire, 2012). These data show that execution times for a strategy on a given problem were increased for both young and older participants if they had executed a difficult strategy on the previous problem.

strategy (rounding up) than to execute an easier strategy (such as rounding down). After executing the most resource-demanding strategy, fewer resources were available to execute the required strategy on the following item, leading to increased latencies. What was interesting about these data was that strategy sequential difficulty effects were similar in young and older participants. It was as if young and older adults had the same need for more time to execute a strategy after using a difficult strategy than after an easier one (see also Uittenhove & Lemaire, 2013a, b; Uittenhove, Poletti, Dufau, & Lemaire, 2013). The equivalence of sequential difficulty effects between young and older adults seen here in arithmetic problem solving has also been found in another domain, namely episodic memory (Uittenhove, Burger, Taconnat, & Lemaire, 2015).

In sum, older adults' strategy execution seems to be more affected by sequential effects than that of young adults, as increased strategy switch costs and the sequential modulations of the poorer-strategy effect show. But it is important to note that not all sequential effects increase with age (e.g., strategy sequential difficulty effects).

Conclusions

Basic research in cognitive psychology has shown that participants' performance (i.e., speed, accuracy) on a cognitive task depends on the type of strategy they use. Such work has also shown that the speed at which a strategy is executed depends on the number and type of mental procedures involved in each strategy. Finally, research in this area has revealed that these mental procedures are affected by parameters such as stimulus type and the characteristics of the situation and the participants. This means that a given strategy can be executed more rapidly than another when it is used to solve one type of problem (or in one particular situation), and more slowly on a different type of problem (or in a different situation).

Research in the psychology of aging has shown that, in many cognitive domains, aging is accompanied by change in how a given strategy is executed (Table 5.1). The results of these studies have also shown that the effects of age on strategy execution are modulated by the factors that affect strategy implementation, such as problem and situational characteristics. Differences between young and older participants vary with the strategy used (i.e., young adults may execute one type of strategy more quickly than older adults, while with another type they may be slower or there may be no performance difference). These differences are

TABLE 5.1 A nonexhaustive list of studies showing change in strategy execution during aging

Cognitive domain	Type of task used	Study
Visual attention	Detection of changes in visual scenes	Costello et al., 2012; Veiel, Storandt, & Abrams, 2006
Numerical cognition	Complex addition-solving tasks	Allen et al., 1992, 1997; 2005; Geary & Wiley, 1991
	Complex addition-solving tasks	Green et al., 2007
	Complex multiplication-solving tasks	Siegler & Lemaire, 1997
	Computational estimation tasks	Ardiale et al., 2012; Lemaire & Hinault, 2014; Lemaire et al., 2004; Uittenhove & Lemaire, 2012, 2013a, b
Spatial cognition	Spatial navigation on graphical tablets	Arning & Ziefle, 2009
Language	Text reading with the moving-window technique	Paterson, McGowan, & Jordan, 2013
Episodic memory	Word-pair learning task	Dunlosky & Hertzog, 2001
	Isolated-word learning task	Dirkx & Craik, 1992; Froger, Taconnat, Landré, Beigneux, & Isingrini,, 2009; Naveh-Benjamin, Craik, Guez, & Kreuger, 2005
	Implicit memory task (word-stem completion)	Osorio et al., 2010
Working memory	Sternberg scanning task	Rypma, Berger, Genova, Rebbech, & D'Esposito, 2005
	Olfactory recognition task	Moberg & Raz, 1997
Decision making	Fishing task	Mata et al., 2009 von Helversen & Mata, 2012

modulated by the type of problem to be solved and the situation in which participants perform the task.

Generally speaking, it seems that the more processing resources an experimental condition requires, the larger the age-related performance differences. The more difficult the strategy and/or the problem, or the more constraining the situation in which the task is performed, the greater the strategy performance difference between young and older adults. In other words, variations in the effects of aging on participants' cognitive performance depend on the relative difficulty of the strategies they use. The execution times of strategies that include more processing steps or that require more processing resources increase more with aging. But these effects of relative difficulty are modulated by stimulus, situational, and task characteristics. This suggests that, to explain performance differences between young and older participants, it is important to take strategy differences into account. Taking into account the context in which the strategies are executed also seems to be crucial.

6

AGING AND STRATEGY SELECTION

Chapter outline

Aging and strategy flexibility
Aging and the ability to select the best strategy
Aging and the calibration of strategy choices to task parameters
Conclusions

Even if aging is not accompanied by changes in strategy repertoire, distribution, or execution, the strategy selection mechanisms of young and older adults may differ at several levels. For example, young and older adults' choice of which strategy to use to solve each problem might be based on different problem features. At the empirical level, this is apparent when percentage of use of different strategies is influenced by one stimulus characteristic in one group and by a different characteristic in another group. Another way that strategy selection might vary with aging is if young and older adults' choice of which strategy to use on each problem is based on the same stimulus characteristics, but the strength of these characteristics' respective influence on strategy choices differs with aging. The efficacy of strategy selection mechanisms might also decline if older participants are less able to calibrate their strategy choices to the constraints of the testing situation or the task. And finally, aging might lead to a deterioration of the ability to select the best strategy for each problem. Researchers have reported findings from many situations suggesting that strategy selection mechanisms become less efficacious during aging. It has also been shown that this decrease in strategy selection with aging is not due to a deterioration of strategy flexibility in older adults. To the contrary, a host of studies have shown that older adults can maintain a certain strategy flexibility, a necessary condition for efficient strategy selection. That is, they are able to change strategy from one item to the next, rather than staying rigidly attached to one strategy, systematically using it for all items. Here we look at a few examples of studies that found evidence of strategy flexibility in older adults, followed by findings showing decreasing strategy selection performance with age.

Aging and strategy flexibility

One of the first prerequisites to studying the relationship between age and strategy selection is making sure that older participants are in fact able to select a strategy to use on each item, rather than choosing to perform a given task exclusively with a single strategy. Research on strategy repertoire and distribution (see Chapters 2 and 3) has shown that this is the case. The next step is to make sure that they show some degree of strategy flexibility. Empirically this can be seen, for example, if older participants are able to change their strategy choices when explicitly asked to do so and/or when task constraints lead them to do so in order to improve their performance. A number of empirical findings have shown that older adults are able to adjust their strategy choices as a function of explicit or implicit task constraints.

Induced strategy adjustments: The example of episodic memory

In an experiment on episodic memory, Dunlosky and Hertzog (1998) asked young and older participants to memorize 30 related word pairs (e.g., *king–crown*). The participants were tested in two conditions. In the first, the experimenter told the participants that they could use whichever strategy they wanted to memorize each word pair. In the second condition, participants had to try to generate a mental image as often as possible (e.g., imagining a king wearing a crown on his head). After the memorization phase, the participants performed a cued recall test: They were shown the first word in each word pair and had to give the second word in response. When the authors analyzed the percentages of items on which the participants reported using the various available strategies (see Figure 6.1 for mental imagery), they found that both young and older participants significantly increased their use of mental imagery (and decreased their use of other strategies) in the condition where they were instructed to do so. In other words, the two groups adjusted similarly to pressure created by the instruction to try and use mental imagery to encode related word pairs. The importance of this result is that it demonstrates the existence of a degree of strategy flexibility (i.e., the ability to change strategies, rather than sticking to a single strategy on all items) in older adults. This suggests that, if aging is accompanied by a decrease in the ability to adapt strategy selection to task constraints, the explanation is not always mental rigidity or a lack of flexibility that develops during aging. It could always be argued, however, that in reality the participants in Dunlosky and Hertzog's (1998) experiment were not spontaneously adapting to the situation, but simply obeying instructions to

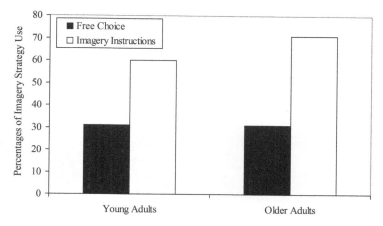

FIGURE 6.1 Percentages of use of mental imagery to memorize word pairs by young and older adults, according to the task instructions (data from Dunlosky & Hertzog, 1998). These data show that young and older adults significantly and similarly increased their use of mental imagery when encouraged to do so by the task instructions.

execute a particular strategy. This means that these findings in themselves are not enough to show that age spared the participants' ability to change their own strategy (toward using the most effective strategy, mental imagery) according to the situation, since the task instructions explicitly asked them to make this change, and they were simply complying.

Spontaneous strategy adjustments: The example of decision making

In a study on decision making, Mata and colleagues (Mata, Schooler, & Rieskamp, 2007) found that young and older adults made similar spontaneous strategy changes according to the situation. In their experiment, 83 young participants and 86 older participants were given the task of deciding which of two diamonds (A or B) was more expensive (the procedure is illustrated in Figure 6.2). The diamonds were characterized by eight variables, or cues, such as size (small or large), clarity (clear or cloudy), color (colored or uncolored). Each trial began with a set of four boxes on a touchscreen, two for each diamond: One button to request information on each diamond, and the other to display the information. A question was displayed in the middle of the screen: "Which diamond do you want to find out more about?" After one of the two buttons at the bottom of the touchscreen had been touched, some information was revealed about the corresponding diamond in the box above (e.g., the fact that it was a large diamond). The information appeared for a duration of 2 seconds and then disappeared. The participant then touched one of the two buttons again (either the same box for more information about the same diamond,

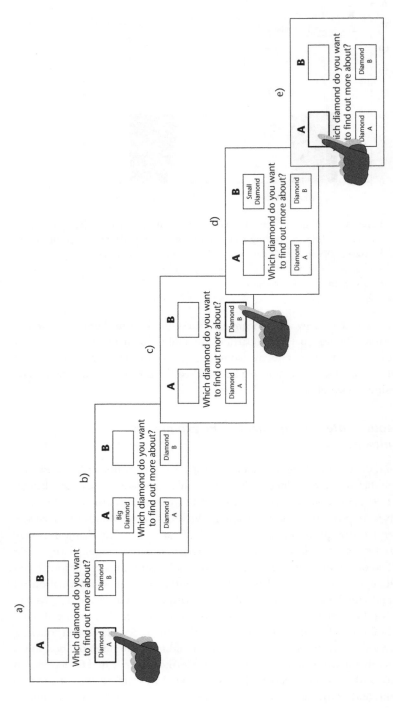

FIGURE 6.2 Procedure in the diamond task used by Mata et al. (2007) to study decision-making strategies and aging (see text for further details). (Reprinted from Mata, R., R., Schooler, L. J., & Rieskamp, J. (2007). The aging decision maker: Cognitive aging and the adaptive selection of decision strategies. *Psychology and Aging, 22*(4), 796–810, APA, with permission.)

or the other button for more information about the other diamond), information again appeared in the corresponding box for 2 seconds, and so on until the participant decided which of the two diamonds was more expensive. Participants could make their decision at any time (i.e., regardless of how much information they had uncovered about either or both of the diamonds).

The participants were tested in two conditions. In the first condition, the so-called equal-validities condition, each of the eight cues was equally valid (71%). If size had a validity of 71%, this meant that the larger of the two diamonds was more expensive in 71 of 100 cases (or, in other words, that simply choosing the larger of the two diamonds meant that the participant had a 71% chance of choosing correctly). In the second condition, the first cue that the participants obtained was the most valid (81%), the second cue the second-most valid (71%), the third cue the third-most valid (69%), and so on down to the eighth and final cue (whose validity was 54%). In other words, in the second condition the cues were presented in descending order of validity. The participants were informed of the cues' validity in both conditions.

Using a classification algorithm based on the participants' performance and the information search parameters (e.g., number of cues examined, searches for several cue values for a single diamond vs. successive comparisons of the two diamonds), Mata et al. were able to determine whether each participant mainly used a weighted additive rule (WADD) strategy, a Take The Best (TTB) strategy, or a Take Two strategy. Participants using a WADD strategy would try to take all variables into account on most trials, weighting them by their validity. Participants using the TTB strategy would decide based on a single high-validity cue (e.g., if size was a high-validity cue, they would choose the large diamond). And finally, participants using the Take Two strategy would make their decision as soon as two successive cues favored one of the two diamonds (e.g., after two successive screens revealed that Diamond A was larger and Diamond B cloudy, the participant would choose A).

Note that the WADD strategy is the most effective in the equal-validities condition, since the criteria straightforwardly compensate for (overrule) one another in case of invalidity, and using the maximum number of criteria leads to the best decision. The TTB and Take Two strategies, on the other hand, are better adapted to an environment with unequal cue validities, since in this case lower-validity cues are not as likely to compensate for earlier, higher-validity cues, offering an incentive to use a less information-intensive strategy.

Despite being more likely to use the easier strategies (Take Two, TTB) overall, older participants were as successful at adapting their strategy choices to condition changes as young participants. The data (Figure 6.3) showed that the proportion of young participants who chose the WADD strategy decreased from 86% in the equal-validities condition to 61% in the unequal-validities condition, versus 66% to 41% in older adults. Meanwhile, the proportion of young participants who used the TTB or Take Two strategies increased from 14% in the equal-validities condition to 36% in the unequal-validities condition (the corresponding percentages for older adults were 32% and 57%).

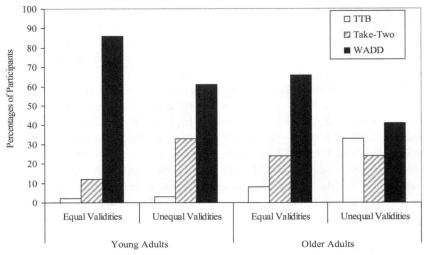

FIGURE 6.3 Number of participants who used each of the three decision-making strategies, by validity condition, in Mata et al. (2007). The data show that the same numbers of young and older participants used the weighted additive (WADD) strategy (vs. one of the other two strategies) less frequently in the unequal-validities condition than in the equal-validities condition. TTB, Take The Best.

Here again, as in the study of Dunlosky and Hertzog (1998) on episodic memory, what is interesting about the findings of Mata et al. (2007) on decision making is their demonstration of a relatively high degree of strategy flexibility in older adults. This combination of observations—an overall difference in strategy preferences (i.e., older adults used the easier decision-making strategies more often than young adults) and an equivalent tendency in the two age groups to vary strategy selection depending on the experimental context—confirmed the need to distinguish (at least in the domain of decision making) between different aspects of strategy, such as preferences (or distribution) and selection. However, this study is subject to two limitations. First, although each participant saw 50 decision problems, because the experiment and the data analyses were based on categorizing each participant according to a single dominant strategy, this approach did not allow the authors to determine whether each individual in fact used just one strategy to solve all 50 problems. The approach also rules out the possibility of sensitive testing for age-related differences in strategy selection, as reflected, for example, by differences in strategy distribution between conditions (equal vs. unequal validities, in the study of Mata et al.). When possible, assessing the strategy used on each item is a far preferable approach. This approach shows whether individuals use multiple strategies to perform a given task (thus offering more precise information about what participants really do when they carry it out), reveals the relative frequencies with which they do so, and, importantly, allows experimenters to examine how strategy frequencies vary between experimental conditions. In other words, it is both a more valid and a more sensitive way to study the effects of aging on strategy selection.

Aging and the ability to select the best strategy

Changes with age in the ability to select the best strategy on each item have been studied both directly (by explicitly asking participants to select the best strategy for each item) and indirectly (e.g., by instructing participants to perform as well as possible). Effects of aging have been reported with both approaches.

Direct studies of the effects of aging on the selection of the best strategy

In a series of studies on changes with aging in our ability to select the best strategy, a group of collaborators and I (e.g., Hodzik & Lemaire, 2011; Lemaire, Arnaud, & Lecacheur, 2004) gave computational estimation tasks to young and older participants. In these tasks, the participants were shown multiplication problems with two two-digit numbers, such as 43 × 68, and had to choose one of the available strategies to estimate the product of the two numbers that yielded the most accurate result. On each problem participants had to choose whether to use a rounding-down strategy (i.e., rounding the two operands down to the nearest decade; e.g., using 40 × 60 to estimate 43 × 68) or a rounding-up strategy (i.e., rounding the two operands up to the nearest decades; e.g., computing 50 × 70). The participants had to choose the best of these two strategies. On some problems, choosing the best strategy was very easy (e.g., 43 × 54; 37 × 89), given that either both of the unit digits were larger than 5 or both were smaller than 5. It was much more difficult to choose the best strategy on other problems (e.g., 47 × 63; 24 × 76) wherein one each of the unit digits was respectively larger and smaller than 5. The participants were not allowed to use a mixed-rounding strategy (i.e., rounding one of the operands down to the nearest decade and the other up to the nearest decade), in order to make strategy selection more difficult and thus maximize the probability of observing age-related differences in the selection of the best strategy. As seen in the results of the two studies summarized in Figure 6.4 (see also Barulli, Rakitin, Lemaire, & Stern, 2013), older participants were less likely to select the best strategy on each problem. Note that, in all of these studies, older participants' level of expertise in mental calculation was either equivalent to or higher than that of young participants. Any age-related decline in the ability to select the best strategy thus could not be due to a lower baseline ability to perform mental calculations in older participants.

In several studies on episodic memory, Alan Castel and his colleagues examined age-related differences in how participants select most crucial information to remember. In their paradigm, called selectivity paradigm, participants are given lists of words to memorize. Each word is associated with points, such that participants receive more points for correctly recalled highest-value words and fewer points for lowest-value words. Participants are instructed to recall as many words as possible

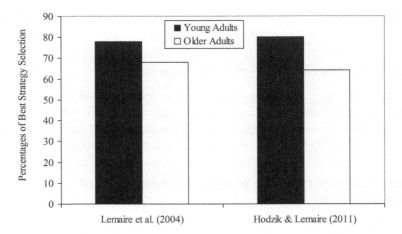

FIGURE 6.4 Mean percentage use of the best strategy in two studies requiring young and older participants to choose the best strategy on each problem in order to estimate the product of two two-digit numbers (data from Lemaire et al., 2004, and Hodzik & Lemaire, 2011).

but also to obtain the largest number of points. From these two measures, number of correctly recalled words, and number of total points earned, it is possible to quantify all participants' ability to strategically focus their attention at encoding to highest-value words and examine age-related differences in this selectivity. This is an important issue because all information we need to memorize is not equally important or crucial. In fact, more generally, among all pieces of information we need to process, some are more important than others, and it is crucial that we allocate largest amounts of attentional resources to most crucial information. For example, Figure 6.5 shows mean number of correctly recalled words and selectivity index in young, middle-aged, and older adults. In this experiment, Castel et al. (2011) presented lists of 12 words to memorize. Each word was paired with a

(a)

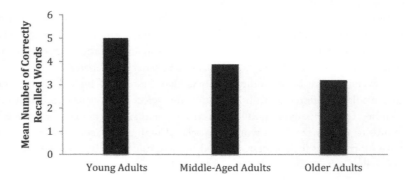

(b)

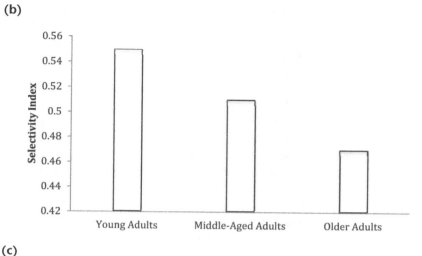

(c)

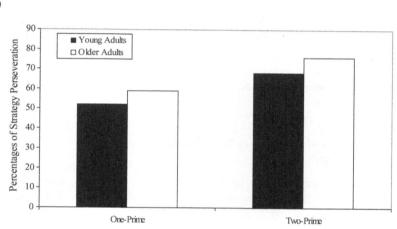

FIGURE 6.5 Decreased number of correctly recalled words (a) and of selectivity index (b) with age (data from Castel et al., 2011). These results show that older adults are less able to select the highest-value words while encoding a series of words for a subsequent memory test. (c) Percentage of strategy repetitions from one problem to the next in young and older adults in one-prime and two-prime conditions (data from Lemaire & Leclère, 2014a).

number (i.e., a point value) ranging from 1 to 12. The larger the number, the more important was the word to remember. Each word and its number were displayed on the computer screen for 2 seconds. As can be seen in Figure 6.5, increased age was accompanied with lower recall and selectivity scores. These results have been found several times (e.g., Castel, 2005; 2008; Castel, Balota, & McCabe, 2009; Castel, Benjamin, Craik, & Watkins, 2002; Castel, Farb, & Craik, 2007). Decreased lower selectivity with increasing age revealed that, as participants grow older, they are less and less able to strategically select the most crucial information to remember.

The mechanisms underlying age-related decreases in participants' skills at selecting the best strategy are still unclear. Some recent studies suggest that decline with age in our ability to select the best strategy results notably from decreases in processing resources, whether in information-processing speed or in other resources such as executive functions (e.g., Bouazzaoui et al., 2010; Duverne & Lemaire, 2004; Frank, Touron, & Hertzog, 2013; Hertzog, Touron, & Hines, 2007; Hodzik & Lemaire, 2011; Touron & Hertzog, 2009). This decline is thus markedly smaller in older people who have maintained relatively high information-processing speed, or whose executive functions (e.g., inhibition, working-memory updating) continue to work at a very high level. For example, while Hodzik and Lemaire (2011) found that age explained 18% of the variance in how likely participants were to select the best strategy in a computational estimation task, this percentage decreased to 11% after executive functions such as inhibition and cognitive flexibility were taken into account. This means that 39% of age-related variance in the selection of the best strategy on this computational estimation task was mediated by executive functions. In the domain of episodic memory, Bouazzaoui et al. (2010) found that 82% of age-related variance in the use of so-called internal strategies (e.g., mental repetition) was explained by executive functions. Note that, while it may be the case that executive functions' mediating role in age effects on strategy selection varies between domains, this hypothesis has not yet been empirically confirmed.

Indirect studies of aging effects on the selection of the best strategy

Studies on inter-item and intra-item strategy switching have also found decreases with age in the ability to select the best strategy. Studies on inter-item strategy switching investigate whether participants tend to repeat the same strategy from one item to the next, or whether they readily change strategies as the problem requires. In studies on intra-item strategy switching, researchers investigate participants' ability to revise their initial strategy choices on a given item, changing strategies some time after they have begun to execute one strategy in order to solve the problem with another, more effective strategy.

For example, in Lemaire and Leclère (2014a), we gave young and older participants a computational estimation task wherein they had to estimate the product of two two-digit numbers (e.g., 43 × 58) using either a rounding-down strategy (i.e., 40 × 50 = 2,000) or a rounding-up strategy (i.e., 50 × 60 = 3,000). We gave participants sets of three successive problems in two different conditions. In the first condition, the so-called one-prime condition, the participants were shown a prime problem (e.g., 31 × 72) followed by a target problem (e.g., 43 × 67), followed by a post-target problem (e.g., 23 × 81). In the second condition, the so-called two-prime condition, the participants were shown two prime problems (e.g., 31 × 72, 23 × 81) followed by a target problem (e.g., 43 × 67). The question was whether the participants would re-use the strategy they had used on the prime problem(s) on the target problem in each trial.

The data (Figure 6.5c) showed that older participants had a stronger tendency to repeat the same strategy from one item to the next than young participants, both in the one- and two-prime conditions. This was the case even on problems where changing strategy would have enabled the participant to use the best strategy. It is as if older adults had more difficulties inhibiting the strategy they had just used on one problem in order to use a different strategy on the next.

A series of studies on intra-item strategy changes also demonstrated this phenomenon of older adults having difficulties changing strategy in order to select the best strategy. The question in these studies is whether, once participants have selected and partly executed a strategy, they are able to revise their initial strategy choice, switching during its execution to another, better strategy. In a series of experiments, Ardiale and Lemaire (2012, 2013) presented young and older participants with a problem such as 42 × 56 along with the strategy to be executed (e.g., rounding-up, in this case solving 50 × 60 = 3,000). Participants had to execute the indicated strategy (either the rounding-down strategy or the rounding-up strategy) for 1,000 ms. After 1,000 ms, the problem appeared again with no indication of which strategy to use, and the participants had the option of changing strategy if they thought that the one they were executing was not the best for the problem. The initially indicated strategy was the better one on half the problems (in which case the right choice was to continue with the same strategy) and the poorer one on the other half of the problems (in which case the right choice was to switch strategies). Determining the best strategy was easy (e.g., 42 × 51 or 68 × 39) on some problems and difficult on other problems (e.g., 42 × 59). As the data presented in Figure 6.6 show, older participants had more difficulty revising their strategy choices in order to use the best strategy on each problem. On problems where determining which strategy was the best was difficult (e.g., 42 × 59), older participants were significantly less likely than young participants to change strategies after beginning to execute the poorer strategy.

This age-related decrease in intra-item strategy switching could not be due to deteriorated mental calculation processes in older adults (since independent testing showed that their mental calculation abilities were either matched or superior to those of the younger participants) nor to an inability to change strategies after beginning to execute one due to mental rigidity (since they were as likely to change strategies as young participants when selecting the best strategy was easy: e.g., 42 × 53). Difficult problems likely require more cognitive resources, notably in order to analyze the features, such as the size of the units, which play a key role in determining the best strategy. Because cognitive resources decrease with age, it may be that older participants did not have enough resources available to switch strategies as often as necessary on difficult problems, in contrast to young participants. In a second study (Ardiale & Lemaire, 2013), we showed that changing the duration of the initial period of strategy execution to 2 or 3 seconds (possibly, we reasoned, allowing older adults more time to analyze the characteristics of the

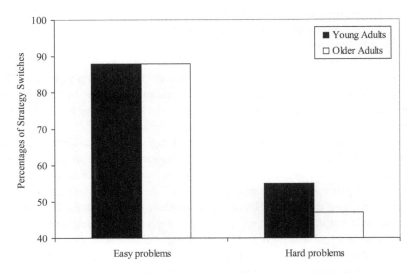

FIGURE 6.6 Percentage of strategy switches in young and older participants when the initially selected strategy was the poorer strategy, according to the difficulty of determining the best strategy (based on Ardiale & Lemaire, 2012). These data show that, when the best strategy for the problem was difficult to determine, older adults had more difficulties revising their initial strategy choice than young adults.

problems) made no difference: Older participants continued to switch strategies less frequently than young participants, even when the initially selected strategy was the poorer one.

Aging and the calibration of strategy choices to task parameters

Change with age in our ability to adjust our strategy choices to different task parameters has been studied in many cognitive domains, using a variety of tasks. These studies have looked at the effects of item, situation, and task characteristics.

Age × item characteristics

A number of studies have sought to determine whether young and older adults differ in their ability to adjust their strategy choices to item types. For example, in a study on episodic memory conducted by Tournier and Postal (2011), each participant was shown 39 word pairs on a computer screen for 8 seconds each. The participants were instructed to memorize each pair for later recall, and were told that they could use whichever strategy they thought best for each word pair. Before performing the task, they were informed of the different available strategies (i.e., mental repetition, mental imagery, sentence generation, etc.) and of their relative efficacy. After the learning phase, the participants were shown the first word in each pair and had to provide the second. They also had to indicate which strategy they had used.

Analyses of strategy selection (Figure 6.7) revealed that older adults were less able to adjust their strategy choices to stimulus characteristics. For example, with concrete words, older people less often used the most effective strategy (i.e., creating mental images) than young people: They used this strategy on 65% of concrete word pairs, versus 83% among young participants. This age difference was also observed (albeit to a lesser extent) for abstract words, with which young and older adults used sentence generation in 49% and 38% of cases, respectively.

Age × task type

The type of task participants perform can influence age-related differences in how they calibrate their strategy choices to the types of problems they have to solve. For example, in 2001, colleagues and I carried out a series of studies on currency conversion. We took advantage of the transition to the euro in France to study the strategies that young and older adults used to convert French francs into euros and vice versa. After studying the different available conversion strategies (Lemaire, Lecacheur, Ferréol-Barbey, 2001; Masse, Lecacheur, & Lemaire, 2000), we performed an experiment where we asked young and older participants to convert amounts given in French francs into euros and the reverse

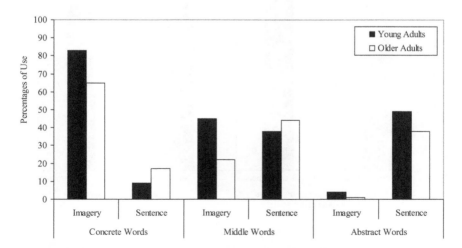

FIGURE 6.7   Percentage of word pairs memorized using mental imagery and sentence generation by young and older participants (data from Tournier & Postal, 2011). These data show that older participants less often used the strategy that was better adapted to each item type than young participants.

(Lemaire & Lecacheur, 2001). Some of the amounts were small (e.g., 32 francs; 27 euros) while others were larger (e.g., 68 francs; 93 euros). In the francs-to-euros conversion task, the participants could choose to use one of two strategies to convert each amount: The so-called add-half strategy (i.e., divide the amount by 2, add this quotient to the amount, and divide the resulting sum by 10; e.g., 60 francs = 60/2 = 30; 30 + 60 = 0; 90/10 = 9 euros), or the so-called multiply-by-three strategy (i.e., multiply the amount by 3, divide the product by 2, and divide by 10; e.g., 60 francs = 60×3 = 180; 180/2 = 90; 90/10 = 9 euros). In the euros-to-francs conversion task, the participants could also choose between two strategies to convert each amount: The so-called divide-by-three strategy (i.e., divide the amount by 3, multiply this quotient by 2, and then multiply the resulting product by 10: e.g., 120 euros = 120/3 = 40; 40 × 2 = 80; 80 × 10 = 800 francs), or the so-called multiply-by-six strategy (i.e., multiply the amount by 6 and add 10% to this product: e.g., 50 euros = 50 × 6 = 300; 300 + 30 = 330 francs).

As the data in Figure 6.8 show, strategy selection differences between young and older adults varied with the type of conversion. When they had to convert small amounts of francs into euros, older participants used the add-half strategy less often

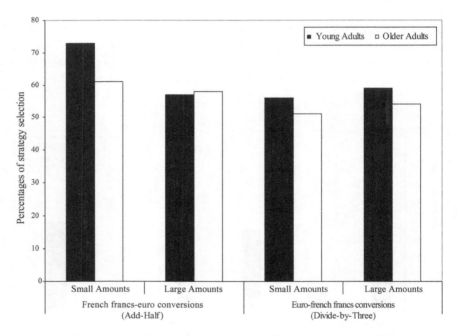

FIGURE 6.8 Percentages of trials where young and older participants used the add-half strategy in a francs-to-euros conversion task and the divide-by-three strategy in a euros-to-francs conversion task, with small and large amounts (data from Lemaire & Lecacheur, 2001). These data show that differences between young and older adults in strategy selection interacted with the conversion task and the amount to be converted.

than young participants, whereas the two groups were equally likely to select this strategy when converting larger amounts. When converting euros into francs, older adults used the divide-by-three strategy less often than young adults with both small and large amounts. In sum, the results of this study on currency conversion showed that the effects of stimulus type and task interacted differently in young and older adults.

Age × situation type

These two studies, on currency conversion (Lemaire & Lecacheur, 2001) and memory encoding (Tournier & Postal, 2011), show that our abilities to calibrate our strategy choices to the characteristics of items and tasks change with age. This is also true of our ability to calibrate our strategy choices to situational constraints. This type of calibration is seen in how participants' strategy choices vary when they are asked to solve easy and difficult problems as quickly as possible in either time-limited or time-unlimited conditions. In Lemaire et al. (2004), we asked 96 young adults and 96 older adults to perform a computational estimation task, finding the approximate products of pairs of two-digit numbers (e.g., 34×68). The participants had to choose between a rounding-down strategy and a rounding-up strategy. The rounding-down strategy consisted of rounding the two operands down to the nearest decade (e.g., calculating $30 \times 60 = 1,800$ to estimate the product of 34×68). The rounding-up strategy consisted of rounding the two operands up to the nearest decades (e.g., calculating $40 \times 70 = 2,800$). The participants had to solve rounding-down problems, where the rounding-down strategy provided a more accurate estimate (e.g., 36×62), and so-called rounding-up problems, where the rounding-up strategy yielded a better estimate (e.g., 27×64). Finally, the participants were tested in one condition where the instructions emphasized accuracy (i.e., the participants were told that they should provide estimates that were as close as possible to the exact product) and in another condition where accuracy was not emphasized. We looked at how age-related differences in how participants chose between the rounding-down strategy and the rounding-up strategy varied depending on the problem to be solved and as a function of accuracy emphasis.

The data (Figure 6.9) showed that accuracy emphasis modulated the age difference in the frequency with which participants chose the rounding-down strategy on each problem type. When accuracy was not emphasized, the difference between young and older participants in the likelihood of using the rounding-down strategy was the same on both rounding-down problems and rounding-up problems. But when the experimenter asked the participants to try and answer as accurately as possible, young participants were considerably more likely than older participants to use the most appropriate strategy for a given problem. In other words, change with age in our ability to calibrate our strategy choices to the type of item, task, or situation is not additive. On the contrary, these parameters interact during cognitive aging.

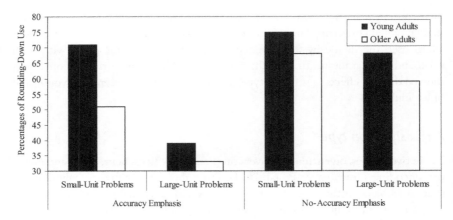

FIGURE 6.9 Percentage of use of the rounding-down strategy to estimate rounding-down problems (e.g., 26 × 71) and rounding-up problems (e.g., 68 × 34) in a situation with or without accuracy emphasis (data from Lemaire et al., 2004). The data show that the strategy choices of young and older participants were differently affected by the problem type and accuracy emphasis.

Age × item type × task type × situation

Interactions between age, problem type, situational characteristics, and tasks are not restricted to the domain of arithmetic problem solving: They have also been documented in other domains of cognition. For example, in a study on encoding in episodic memory, Froger, Bouazzaoui, Isingrini, and Taconnat (2012) found that age-related differences in strategy selection interact with item and situational characteristics. They asked young and older participants to learn lists of word pairs. The words in each pair were either strongly associated (e.g., *dolphin–aquarium*) or weakly associated (e.g., *pyramid–aquarium*). The participants were tested in two encoding conditions. The encoding time was either fixed (i.e., each word pair was presented for 6 seconds) or self-paced (i.e., the participants could take whatever amount of time they wanted to encode each word pair). Finally, participants were tested in three conditions where they were given three different levels of information about the strategies. Participants in the control condition were given no information about the strategies. In the second (low environmental support) condition, they were given minimal information (i.e., the available strategies were simply listed). And finally, in the third (high environmental support) condition, the participants were given more information about the different strategies: Not only were the strategies listed, but their relative effectiveness was described (e.g., the experimenter told the participants that mental imagery was a more effective strategy than sentence generation, which in turn was more effective than mental repetition). After the encoding phase, the participants performed a cued-recall test (i.e., they saw the first word in each word pair and had to recall the second word). In addition to performance measures (e.g., percentage of correctly recalled items), the authors analyzed the selection of the three encoding strategies (which they probed immediately following the encoding of each word pair). They analyzed the use of these strategies in each age group and its relationship to the encoding condition, the type of item, and the information the participants were given about the strategies (environmental support).

The data shown in Figure 6.10 clearly revealed an Age × Encoding Time × Environmental Support × Strength of Association interaction on how often participants selected each of the three main strategies (imagery, sentences, and repetition).

(a)

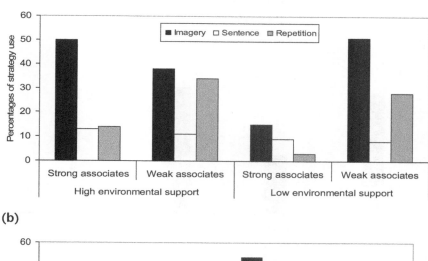

(b)

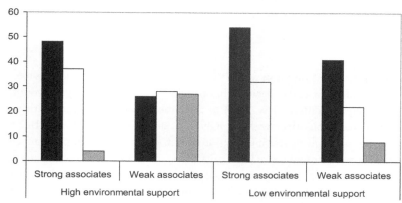

FIGURE 6.10 Young and older adults' percentage use of the three main strategies, by encoding condition and type of items (data from Froger et al., 2012). These results show how the effects of age, stimulus characteristics, and task context interact in modulating strategy selection in an episodic memory task.

(c)

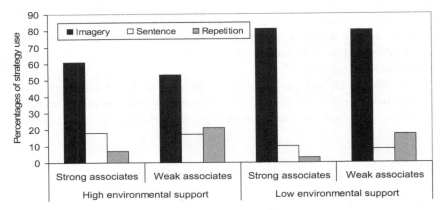

(d)

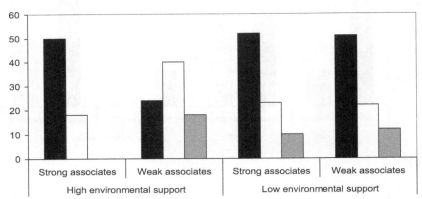

FIGURE 6.10 (*continued*)

For example, in the condition where the participants determined their own encoding time and were given detailed information about the strategies, young and older participants differed less (11%) in their use of mental imagery with weakly associated word pairs than with strongly associated word pairs (29%). But when participants were given less information about the strategies, this difference was comparable with strongly associated pairs (31%) and weakly associated pairs (29%). When the encoding duration was fixed at 6 seconds per pair, a different pattern of differences between young and older adults was found. In the condition where they were given detailed information on the strategies, young and older participants used mental imagery with equal frequency on strongly associated pairs, whereas on weakly associated pairs older participants used this strategy slightly less often than young adults. When the participants were given no information about the strategies, older participants used mental imagery more often on strongly associated pairs and less often on weakly associated pairs. The differences between young and older participants in using the other two strategies (sentence generation and repetition) varied in the same way between the different conditions. In summary, the results of Froger and colleagues (2012) illustrate the complex play of interactions between the variables characterizing the situation, the stimuli, the task, and the participants in the selection of mnemonic strategies, just as in problem solving.

Conclusions

Strategy selection is one of the most original dimensions in the conceptual framework proposed here for the study of age-related differences in strategic variations. In this chapter we have seen that, as with other strategy dimensions, even for a given task and within a single cognitive domain, the strategy selection of young and older adults can sometimes differ and sometimes be similar. When a difference is found, older adults less often choose the best strategy for each item, and calibrate their strategy choices less effectively to task parameters (such as problem and situational characteristics). Effects of aging on strategy selection have been found in many cognitive domains (Table 6.1).

As with other strategy dimensions, it is important for anyone wishing to understand performance differences between young and older adults to take into account how participants select strategies on each item. The first question is whether the effects of different factors on how frequently participants use each strategy change with aging, or remain the same. Next, insofar as some knowledge has been gained on the mechanisms through which these factors influence strategy selection and the

TABLE 6.1 Nonexhaustive list of studies showing changes in strategy selection with aging

Cognitive domain	Type of task used	Study
Numerical cognition	Computational estimation	Ardiale & Lemaire, 2012, 2013; Barulli et al., 2013; Hodzik & Lemaire, 2011; Lemaire & Leclère, 2014a; Lemaire et al., 2004;
	Currency conversion	Lemaire & Lecacheur, 2001
Episodic memory	Paired-associate learning	Tournier & Postal, 2011 Froger et al., 2012
	Single-word learning	Castel, 2005, 2008 Castel et al., 2002, 2007, 2011; Castel, McGillivray, & Friedman, 2012
Decision making	Fishing diamond	Mata et al., 2007
Problem solving	Collaborative everyday problem solving	Strough, McFall, Flinn, & Schuller, 2008

differences between young and older adults, the question is to determine whether it is these mechanisms that are affected by aging and that, consequently, lead to strategy selection differences between young and older adults.

A pattern emerges from the literature on changes in strategy selection with aging: The factors that influence participants' cognitive performance and those that influence their strategy selection are virtually the same. This does not mean that age-related performance variations stem exclusively from changes in strategy selection. It nevertheless seems that when there is a performance difference between young and older adults, there is probably a difference in strategy selection as well. The exact contribution of strategy selection mechanisms to age-related differences in cognitive performance remains to be established by future studies, both in general and within each cognitive domain.

7

CONCLUSIONS AND PERSPECTIVES

Chapter outline

Other types of factors modulating cognitive aging: The example of stereotype threats and prior task success

Aging and cognitive training effects

Aging and relationships between personality and cognition

Aging and relationships between emotions and cognition

Pathological aging and strategy variations

General conclusions

The results discussed in this book illustrate how a strategy perspective can help us understand cognitive aging. As we have seen over the course of the preceding chapters, taking this perspective allows us to pursue the fundamental objectives of the psychology of aging in the most effective possible way. In every domain where it is adopted, the strategy approach leads to a more accurate and detailed picture of changes in cognitive performance with age. This approach tells us not only about what deteriorates with aging and what remains stable, but also about inter-individual differences among older adults (or how aging leads to greater and/ or earlier decline in some people than in others). It also enables us to understand how some individuals sometimes resort to compensation mechanisms to deal with aging. Finally, the strategy perspective is one of the best ways to gain access to the mechanisms underlying changes in cognitive performance during aging.

The results discussed above show that, in many cognitive domains, young and older participants differ in terms of the repertoire of strategies they use (in particular their number and nature), the frequency with which they use each strategy (distribution), their strategy execution (or performance), and their selection (or choice) of which strategy to use on each item. Moreover, these results highlight three broad categories of phenomena. First, within a single individual, cognitive performance on a task can decrease with age in one condition and remain stable in another. Performance can also show no negative effects of age in one or several cognitive domains while declining in others. Next, within a single group of older people with similar demographic and socio-cultural characteristics, large intra- and inter-individual differences can be found, with highly differentiated cognitive aging profiles in different individuals. During aging, some individuals (or even a single individual selectively in particular cognitive domains) manage to create different compensation mechanisms, functional (e.g., resorting more often to the strategy that is easiest for them to execute) and/or neural (e.g., recruiting additional brain areas to execute the selected strategies more effectively). These mechanisms allow them in many cases to improve (or at least limit deterioration in) their performance. In other words, our patterns of performance can change in a highly complex and differentiated fashion as we age. For this reason, it is important to go beyond simple statements such as "Cognitive performance declines with age" or "The more complex and cognitive resource-demanding the task, the more performance declines with age."

A strategy perspective is not incompatible with other perspectives on cognitive aging, such as the theory of cognitive slowing (Salthouse, 1996). Human cognition undergoes both quantitative and qualitative changes with aging. Some qualitative changes result from quantitative changes, as we saw in observations that a narrowing strategy repertoire and decreased ability to select the best strategy are mediated by quantitative factors such as decreased information-processing speed and the decline of cognitive control mechanisms (e.g., Hodzik & Lemaire, 2011).

Thinking about cognitive aging in terms of age-related strategy changes not only provides a more accurate, detailed, and complete description of how performance changes with advancing age, but it also opens up new ways of studying and understanding some other broad characteristics of cognitive aging. As we will see in this chapter, thinking in terms of strategy variations can offer new insights into other factors (e.g., psycho-social factors like stereotype threats) that modulate age-related changes in cognitive performance, cognitive training effects (allowing us to determine whether training allows individuals to remain cognitively alert), the links between aging and personality (i.e., How do the cognitive characteristics of individuals with different personalities change with age?), the links between emotions and cognition during aging (i.e., Do emotions affect the cognition of older adults as much as that of young adults?), and the general question of pathological aging (i.e., Are neurodegenerative diseases better understood if they are analyzed in terms of strategy variations?).

Other types of factors modulating cognitive aging: The example of stereotype threats and prior task success

There are a number of factors influencing age-related changes in human cognition and a much deeper understanding may be gained by adopting a strategy perspective.

To mention just a few of them, aging effects on human cognition have been found to be influenced by a variety of factors such as task interpretation (e.g., Adams, 1991), socio-emotional goals (Carstensen & Turk-Charles, 1994), beliefs about aging effects on cognition (e.g., Hertzog, Lineweaver, & McGuire, 1999), or motivation (e.g., Hess, Rosenberg, & Water, 2001). Two of such factors can illustrate this point, namely stereotype threat and prior task success.

Effects of stereotype threat

For over 10 years now, a number of studies have shown that when older participants are tested under conditions in which aging stereotype (according to which older adults have or should have poorer performance because of aging) is activated, they obtained poorer performance relative to control conditions under which aging stereotype is not activated. For example, Hess, Auman, Colcombe, and Rahhal (2003) asked young and older adults to accomplish a free-recall task. Participants first studied a list of 30 words for 2 minutes and then had to recall as many words as possible. Participants were tested under three conditions—a negative stereotype threat, a positive, or a control nonthreat condition. In the negative threat and no-threat conditions, participants read short passages before taking the memory task. In the negative, stereotype threat condition, the short passage mentioned reinforced the negative threat stereotype (mentioning recent evidence to support the conclusions that, with age, our memory becomes poorer and poorer). In the positive condition, the short passage mentioned recent evidence that contradicted traditional views regarding the negative effects of aging on memory. In the control condition, participants read no passages before the memory experiment. Participants' performance in the memory task can be seen in Figure 7.1.

The data showed no effects of stereotype conditions in young adults. In older adults, it is clear that activating the negative aging stereotype led participants to correctly recall fewer words, as they recalled 44%, 46%, and 58% in the negative, control, and positive conditions, respectively. This effect of stereotype threat has been found in a number of studies where aging stereotype was directly activated (e.g., Hess & Hinson, 2006; Hess, Hinson, Statham, 2004; Levy, 1996; Stein, Blanchard-Fields, & Hertzog, 2002) and has been found to be modulated by a number of task and participant parameters (e.g., it is stronger in young-older adults, aged 60–70 years, than in older-old adults, aged 70+ years and in more highly than less highly educated older adults ; Hess, Hinson, & Hodges, 2009), but also when aging stereotype was activated indirectly (e.g., Hess & Hinson, 2006; Hess et al., 2004).

Effects of prior task success

Lisa Geraci and her colleagues conducted a series of experiments that yielded very interesting and fascinating results in that respect. In brief, they showed that succeeding in one task improves older adults' performance (but not young adults' performance) on a subsequent task, an effect they termed "effects of prior

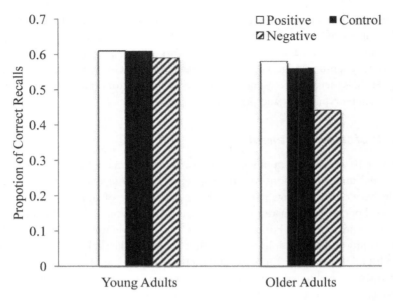

FIGURE 7.1 Proportion of correctly recalled words for young and older adults in each stereotype threat condition (data from Hess et al., 2003). They show that, for older adults only, participants correctly recalled few words in the memory task after being told that recent evidence reinforced age-related decline in memory (i.e., negative stereotype threat condition) than when they were told nothing (control condition) or than when they were told that recent evidence contradicts age-related decline in memory (i.e., positive condition).

task success." These effects of prior success supposedly activated a positive feeling among older adults, counteracting aging stereotype threat. For example, Geraci and Miller (2013) asked 75 young and 75 older adults to accomplish a verbal free-recall task. In this task, participants saw 30 randomly presented words (five words from six different semantic categories; e.g., kitchen utensils) to study for 2 minutes. Then, participants had to recall as many of these words as possible.

Before the memory test, young and older participants were randomly assigned to one of three experimental groups. In the first, group, participants were given 30 sets of five scrambled words. For each set of five words, participants were asked to rearrange the words to form a grammatically correct four-word sentence (e.g., *lamp, the, fell, run, over*). This task was selected because it is known to be easily and successfully accomplished by older adults when participants have no time limits. In this experiment, older adults successfully completed this sentence-scramble task. In the next group, participants were given the same material and the same task but had only 20 seconds to complete the sentence-scramble task (an unrealistic amount of time to accomplish the task successfully). In other words, the first group (called the task success group) successfully accomplished the sentence-scramble task before taking the memory experiment, while the second group failed to do so (this group was called the task failure group). Finally, the third group of participants, the control group, had no task prior to the memory experiment.

The mean proportions of correctly recalled words by young and older participants in each condition are shown in Figure 7.2. It is clear from these data that young participants recalled the same number of words whatever the conditions they were tested in. It is also very clear that older adults, in contrast, were heavily influenced by whether they had successfully accomplished the sentence-scramble task before. Proportions of correct recalls went from 0.39 in control or failure group up to 0.47 in the task success group. At issue here is whether it is enough to be successful at one task before accomplishing another to increase performance on the latter.

Recent data by Geraci and her colleagues (Geraci, Hughes, Miller, & De Forrest, in press) suggest that prior success with any task is not enough. Prior success should occur with a prior task that is related one way or another to the target task. Indeed, older adults obtained similar memory performance (proportion of correct recalls = 0.43) when the memory task followed a noncognitive motor

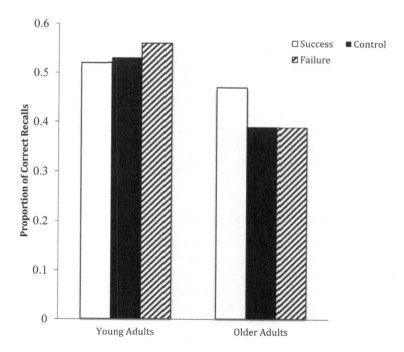

FIGURE 7.2   Proportion of correctly recalled words for young and older adults in each condition (data from Geraci & Miller, 2013). The data show that, for older adults only, participants correctly recalled more words in the memory experiment after they successfully accomplished the sentence-scramble task.

task (i.e., participants were asked to toss beanbags into a bucket placed in front of them) relative to when participants did not accomplish a prior task (proportion of correct recalls = 0.42). In that study, Geraci and her colleagues tested another prior task, a visual search task (i.e., participants saw pictures in which they had to find target objects, e.g., they had to find six chairs in a picture). Interestingly, they found that success in this visual search task facilitated older adults' performance. All in all, it seems that when the prior task is a cognitive task, prior success increases older adults' performance.

One of the issues that the strategy perspective raises about effects of prior task success and age stereotype threat in general concerns the mechanisms through which these effects arise. In the works of Geraci and colleagues, did older adults obtain better performance following task success relative to no prior task success because prior task success led them to use different sets of strategies to accomplish the target memory tasks, or did participants use the same strategies to encode words but executed them more effectively after successfully accomplishing a prior task? Simliarly, in Hess et al.'s and others' work, we do not know if directly activating the stereotype prior to accomplishing the task changed the type of strategies older people use or the way they executed memory strategies while encoding lists of 30 words. Such an issue can be addressed in future works by examining which strategies participants used on each item and how often they used each available strategy in each condition. Such studies could also examine whether prior task success (or stereotype threats) led participants to select the best strategy on each item (e.g., using imagery to encode more concrete words and repetition to encode more abstract words) more (or less) often. Finally, to further understand the effects of prior task success, future studies using the strategy perspective will enable us to determine why the two (prior and current) tasks have to be relatively close (e.g., both tasks have to be cognitive tasks) to generate effects of prior task success. This will be possible because the strategy perspective includes determining the core cognitive processes underlying experimental effects such as effects of prior task success.

Aging and cognitive training effects

Is it possible to counteract the deleterious effects of age on human cognition? In other words, is it possible, using cognitive-training techniques, to improve the cognitive functioning of older adults to the point of delaying and/or slowing (if not actually canceling) performance decline with aging, or even to prevent pathological aging (e.g., Alzheimer's disease (AD))? Numerous research programs have already tested the relative efficacy of some cognitive-training techniques, both in normal aging (see Buitenweg, Murre, & Ridderikhof, 2012, Green & Bavelier, 2008, and Park & Bischof, 2013, for reviews) and in pathological aging (see Sitzer, Twamley, & Jeste, 2006, for a meta-analysis). Moderating effects of cognitive training on performance that decline with aging have been observed many times. These effects are important because they reveal a fundamental characteristic of the aging brain—namely, its plasticity, which can be used to create programs of cognitive stimulation specifically designed for aging. Such effects have been observed at both physiological and cognitive levels. The question that interests us here is whether a strategy perspective can offer a fruitful way to better study and understand these effects.

At the physiological level, a number of studies have found changes in the volume and/or activations of some brain areas with cognitive training. For example, Boyke, Driemeyer, Gaser, Büchel, and May (2008) found an increase in the volume of medial temporal areas (the hippocampus and the nucleus accumbens) in older adults who practiced juggling for 3 months. In another example, Lövdén and colleagues (2013) found that the volume of the hippocampus of older men who played spatial navigation games every 2 days for 4 months did not decrease, whereas the hippocampus of older men who did not play decreased in size. Brehmer et al. (2011) observed decreased frontal activations in older participants who were trained on working-memory tasks. And Nyberg and colleagues (2003) observed increased brain activation in occipito-parietal areas after episodic memory training.

At the level of cognitive performance, researchers have also reported major improvements with cognitive training in older people. Such improvements have been seen in a number of cognitive domains, such as attention (e.g., Bherer & Belleville, 2004a; Ho & Scialfa, 2002), working memory (e.g., Buschkuehl, Jaeggi, Hutchison, Perrig-Chiello, 2008; Li et al., 2008), executive control (Basak, Boot, Voss, & Kramer, 2008; Dahlin, Nyberg, Bäckman, & Stigsdotter Neely, 2008), episodic memory (e.g., Lustig & Flegal, 2008), reasoning (McArdle & Prindle, 2008; Schaie & Willis, 1986), problem solving (e.g., Frank, Touron, & Hertzog, 2013; Touron & Hertzog, 2009), and the acquisition of cognitive abilities (e.g., Onyper, Hoyer, & Cerella, 2008; Rogers, Hertzog, & Fisk, 2000).

The results of the studies of Kliegl, Smith, and Baltes (1989, 1990) illustrate the beneficial effects of cognitive training on memory performance in young and older participants. They compared the performance of 18 young adults (with a mean age of 24 years) to that of 19 older adults (with a mean age of 72 years) on a recall task with a list of 30 words, both before and after cognitive training. This training was based on the method of loci, which the participants trained in for a total of 20 sessions. Before beginning the memory task, the participants first learned to go on a mental trip through a series of historic sites in the city of Berlin. Then, while encoding a list of words, the participants had to visit the sites, always in the same order, creating a distinctive (i.e., "funny, dynamic, or interactive") mental image linking each word in the list with one of the sites. At the time of recall, the participants traveled mentally through the sites once again and retrieved the words associated to each of the corresponding sites. The authors also manipulated the encoding time, presenting each word for a variable duration (e.g., 5, 10, or 20 seconds). The results, which are summarized in Figure 7.3, showed that this training allowed young and older participants to significantly improve their performance. In older adults, the longer the encoding time, the more their performance improved, whereas in young participants encoding time had a smaller effect.

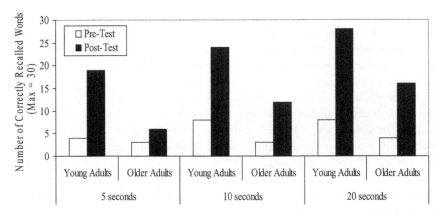

FIGURE 7.3   Number of correctly recalled words in young and older adults before and after training in the method of loci under conditions where participants had 5, 10, or 20 seconds to encode each word (data from Kliegl et al., 1989). These results show that training in the method of loci markedly improved the memory performance of both young and older participants, and that this improvement increased in older adults as encoding time grew.

There are several types of cognitive training, not all of which involve repeating a particular type of exercise many times. Training can also consist, for example, of implementing strategy substitution (i.e., attempting to replace one mode of processing with another, either by direct instruction or indirectly). For example, in a study on deductive reasoning, Takahashi and Overton (1996) attempted to determine whether implementing a more effective reasoning strategy would improve older adults' performance (see also Bherer & Belleville, 2004b, on attention; Brom & Kliegel, 2014, Kliegel & Bürki, 2012, on prospective memory; and Zinke et al., 2014, on working memory). They gave groups of young and older participants eight versions of Wason's (1983; Overton, 1990) famous four-card problem. In these deductive reasoning problems, participants were shown a sentence and four cards. Each card showed information about the consumption of a drink on one side and a person's age on the other. For example, the participants might see the sentence *"If a person is drinking beer, then that person must be over 21,"* along with four cards showing the following elements on their visible side: *"drinking beer," "drinking Coke," "16 years of age,"* and *"21 years of age."* The participants were told that each card had information about what a person was drinking on one side and the person's age on the other side. The participants' task was to say which cards had to be turned over in order to determine whether the rule in the sentence was true or false. The correct response was to attempt to falsify the rule by turning over the cards marked *"beer"* and *"16 years of age"* (formally, turning over the cards p and not q to test this sentence of type $p \rightarrow q$). If *"drinking beer"* was written on the hidden side of the card marked *"16 years of age,"* this would falsify the rule. Similarly, if any age below 21 was marked on the hidden side of the card marked "*drinking beer,*" then the rule would also be falsified.

The interest of Takahashi and Overton's study is that they tested young and older participants in a so-called metacognitive condition, as well as a control condition. In the former, participants had to read aloud the question "*Will this card help me decide if the rule is being broken?*" with each card. In other words, the experimenters tried to induce participants to implement a falsification strategy. In the control condition, the participants did not have to read out this question. As the number of correctly solved problems shows (Table 7.1), the deductive-reasoning performance of older participants in the metacognitive cognition was better than that of those in the control condition, who were not incited to use this falsification strategy. Note, however, that older participants performed worse than young participants in both conditions, and that young participants did not benefit from the metacognitive condition (likely because they already executed this strategy effectively even without being instructed to do so).

Training-induced performance improvements are not restricted to either normal aging or the domain of episodic memory. For example, Belleville and colleagues (2011) also observed such improvements in participants with mild cognitive impairment (MCI), not only in isolated-word learning, but also in learning face–name associations and textual information processing. Over 7 weeks, the authors submitted 17 participants with MCI and nine healthy older control participants to a cognitive-training program focused on a number of functions. The training focused on attentional abilities (visual detection, scanning working memory) and memory abilities (encoding items using various strategies, including mental imagery, the method of loci, and face–name association; text memorization). Pre- and post-training assessments showed substantial cognitive improvements in the three trained functions, in both MCI and older adult control participants (Figure 7.4).

This type of result is very interesting because it demonstrates that older adults' cognitive performance can increase with training in some conditions despite the cognitive decline associated to both normal and pathological aging. The important question that follows is that of mechanisms. Through what mechanisms does cognitive training allow older adults, under some conditions, to significantly increase their cognitive performance and counteract the deleterious effects of age on their intellectual functions? Adopting a strategy perspective may prove extremely useful in answering this question.

Existing research on cognitive training has a number of limitations related to questions of strategy, some of which can be illustrated using the examples just

TABLE 7.1 Mean number of deductive-reasoning problems correctly solved by young and older participants in the control and falsification (metacognitive) conditions

Condition	Young adults	Older adults
Control	2.9	1.1
Falsification	2.8	1.7

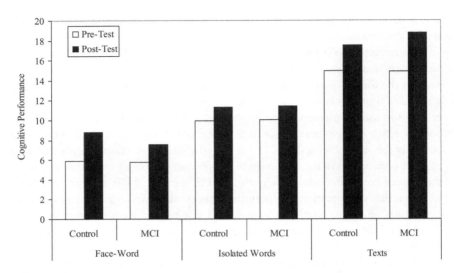

FIGURE 7.4 Performance of participants (older adults with mild cognitive impairment (MCI) and age-matched controls) before and after multi-functional cognitive training (data from Belleville et al., 2011). These results show that the performance of both participants with MCI and controls improved in the three domains tested.

described. For example, Kliegl et al. (1989) found that training had a greater effect in young participants than in older participants. Does this mean that cognitive plasticity decreases with age to the point where older adults no longer enjoy the same cognitive benefits from training as young adults? Before endorsing this conclusion, it is important to establish the answers to several key empirical questions. For example, in the study of Kliegl et al. (1989), did older participants use the method of loci as often as young participants? If not, and young participants used the method of loci on more items than older participants, this alone would be enough for the latter to perform better at post-test. Moreover, did older adults execute the method of loci as efficaciously as young participants? If older participants created weaker associative links between images and sites at encoding time, for example, that too would be enough to make it more difficult for them to retrieve words at the time of recall. Although the researchers took the precaution of training the participants in the method of loci over 20 sessions, increasing the chances that they would use it systematically and execute it efficiently, it remains possible that young and older adults' implementation and/or execution of the strategy differed. Indeed, it is quite likely that out of the 30 words that the participants attempted to recall, young participants used the method of loci more systematically and frequently (i.e., on each item) and executed it more efficiently (i.e., creating strong and distinctive associations between places and words) than older participants. This is possible if the older participants were more likely to attempt to recall the items without thinking back to their site–word associations. Differences in strategy use and execution between young and older participants could result, among other things, from older adults constructing less distinctive site–word associations than young adults at the moment of encoding. In other words, age-related differences in strategy use and execution could underlie the different training effects seen in young and older participants.

In a similar study designed with a strategy perspective in mind, the task and the training could be organized in a way that maximizes the chances that the two groups will use the method of loci at the same frequency and execute it at the highest possible level of efficacy. This is a necessary condition for testing the hypothesis of changes in plasticity with age, all other things being equal. Moreover, a strategy perspective would make it possible to explain observed interactions between age and certain parameters. For example, why did Kliegl et al. (1989) find the effect of presentation duration to be stronger in older participants than in young participants? Could it be because a longer exposure allowed older adults, who are known to have decreased processing speed, to execute the method of loci more effectively? The strategy perspective makes it possible to test this hypothesis directly.

Generally speaking, taking into account the various strategy dimensions discussed above (strategy repertoire, distribution, execution, and selection) should enable us to better understand how cognitive training leads to improvements in both young and older adults. It should also enable us to determine whether strategy changes underlie the physiological changes associated to training, a possibility that has been noted many times by various authors (e.g., Cabeza, Nyberg, & Park, 2005). To take just one example, Park and colleagues noted that, across the neurosciences of aging, "It is also surprisingly difficult to assess whether any observed brain changes reflect a fundamental increase in neural capacity or merely *a change in strategy*" (Park et al., 2013, p. 114, my emphasis). I believe that, with the choice/no-choice method (Siegler & Lemaire, 1997), determining whether strategy changes underlie the changes associated to training becomes a less difficult task.

Aging and relationships between personality and cognition

Many studies have been conducted to try and determine whether there are any links between personality profiles and cognition (see Corr & Matthews, 2009, for an overview). This research is based on a conception of personality as characterized by a certain number of dispositions in thought, feeling, and behavior that are relatively stable over time. These dispositions, or traits, are assessed using personality questionnaires (like the Big Five of Costa & McCrae, 1992). In this type of questionnaire, the participants read a series of statements (e.g., "*I have never literally jumped for joy*"; "*I am easily frightened*"; "*I don't get much pleasure from chatting with people*"). They have to say whether each statement characterizes them, ticking one of the five following responses: "Strongly disagree," "Disagree," "Neutral," "Agree," or "Strongly Agree." Responding "Strongly disagree" means they judge that the statement does not characterize them at all, and "Strongly agree" means they judge that the statement characterizes them very accurately. Different questionnaires include a greater or lesser number of statements (e.g., Costa & McCrae's Neuroticism–Extraversion–Openness Personality Inventory (NEO-PI) includes 240 statements). The statements are constructed (and empirically validated) to assess different dimensions and facets of personality.

A number of theories of personality (and a number of associated questionnaires) have been proposed. One of the best known and most widely used in studies on aging, personality, and cognition is Costa and McCrae's Big Five, with the accompanying NEO-PI questionnaire. According to the Big Five theory, each individual's personality varies in terms of five main trait dimensions:

1. *Neuroticism*: Individuals with a high neuroticism score are anxious, vulnerable, fairly impulsive, and aggressive, or else subject to more or less frequent and intense bouts of depression.
2. *Openness*: Individuals with a high score on this dimension are open to ideas (notably new ideas), connected to their feelings and emotions, as well as to imaginative and esthetic experiences, and have certain values.
3. *Extraversion*: So-called extraverted individuals, those who score high on this dimension, like to be surrounded by a lot of people, engage actively with others, and do not hesitate to assert themselves (or their point of view) in a group; they are also highly active and/or seek out positive emotions.
4. *Conscientiousness*: Individuals with a high score on this dimension have a strong sense of order, a desire to be highly competent and professional in their domain, and a strong sense of duty and success; they are highly disciplined.
5. *Agreeableness:* Individuals who score high on this dimension like to be (and generally are) trusted by others; they are reliable, modest, and sensible; they are also highly altruistic.

Numerous studies have shown that there are systematic links between personality and cognitive performance (see Matthews, 2009, for a review). For example, individuals with high neuroticism scores tend to show lower cognitive performance than those with low neuroticism scores, whereas those who score high on the openness dimension tend to show higher cognitive performance than individuals with lower openness scores (e.g., Moutafi, Furnham, & Paltiel, 2005; Schaie, Willis, & Caskie, 2004; Soubelet & Salthouse, 2011). Another example is that extraverted individuals tend to have higher information-processing speed and greater memory capacity than introverted individuals, but to score lower on reasoning tests (e.g., Graham & Lachman, 2012; McCrae, 1987; Moutafi et al., 2005). So-called agreeable individuals perform less well on tests of reasoning and spatial orientation than less agreeable individuals (Schaie et al., 2004; Willis & Boron, 2008).

Many studies on personality and aging have shown that our personality dimensions and traits remain relatively stable during adulthood, from our 20s or 30s onward (see e.g., Curtis, Windsor, & Soubelet, 2014, Roberts & Del Vecchio, 2000, for reviews). This means that an individual who scores above average for extraversion at age 30 will also tend to be more extraverted than average at age 60 or 70.

Cognition, however, does change with aging. This raises the question of whether the relationships between personality and cognition change or remain stable as we age. Some studies have found evidence suggesting that these links are stable with aging: For example, Soubelet and Salthouse (2011; see also Soubelet, 2011) found that, throughout adulthood, individuals with high scores on items for openness also had good cognitive performance, whereas extraverted individuals tended to have lower levels of cognitive performance. However, many other studies have found that the relationships between personality and cognition tend to change, sometimes in a complex fashion that depends on the personality dimension (or trait) and the cognitive domain examined (e.g., Aiken-Morgan et al., 2012; Baker & Bichsel, 2006; Booth, Schinka, Brown, Mortimer, & Borenstein, 2006; Chamorro-Premuzic, & Furnham, 2003a, b, c; Graham & Lachman, 2014).

For example, Graham and Lachman (2014) administered the NEO-PI and a cognitive battery to 154 adults between the ages of 22 and 84 years. They found a complex pattern of change in the relationships between personality and cognition during aging. What made this study particularly interesting is that, contrary to many other studies, it examined the relationships between personality and cognition not only at the level of dimensions (e.g., neuroticism, agreeableness) but also at the level of traits (e.g., anxiety, depression, vulnerability, and impulsiveness are traits of neuroticism; positive emotions, gregariousness, and assertiveness are traits of extraversion). By separating their group of 154 participants into three subgroups (young adults below age 40, mature adults up to age 60, and older adults), they were able to examine Personality × Cognition interactions in these three age ranges. To assess cognition, they used a cognitive battery developed by Lachman and Tun (2008) called the Brief Test of Adult Cognition by Telephone (BTAC-T). This is a battery of tests which, as its name indicates, can easily be administered by telephone, and which includes tasks assessing verbal fluency (i.e., producing as many names of animals as possible in 1 minute) and inductive reasoning (i.e., indicating which number comes next in a logical sequence such as 3, 6, 9, 12, 15). The other tests in the battery cover information-processing speed, episodic memory, and short-term memory.

Figure 7.5 presents two examples of how the relationships between personality and cognition can evolve during aging. The first concerns a dimension (Neuroticism × Reasoning interaction), the second a trait (Positive Emotions × Verbal Fluency). Figure 7.5a shows that the relationships between neuroticism and reasoning were markedly different in young, and older adults. For example, young individuals with high neuroticism scores had lower reasoning performance than those with lower scores on this dimension. The two levels of neuroticism were associated to equivalent scores in older adults. This results notably from the fact that only individuals with lower neuroticism scores showed a decrease in reasoning abilities with aging (the others, who performed less well at the outset, seemingly had less to lose).

Similarly, Figure 7.5b shows how the relationships between positive emotions (one of the traits of extraversion) and verbal fluency changed with aging. Young people who did not particularly seek out positive emotions had higher verbal

(a)

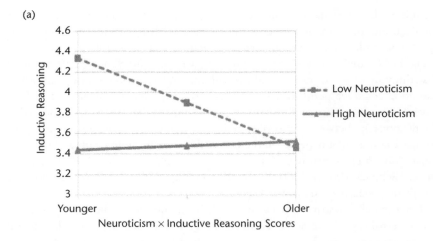

Neuroticism × Inductive Reasoning Scores

(b)

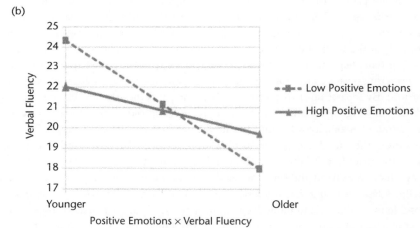

Positive Emotions × Verbal Fluency

FIGURE 7.5 Two examples of change in the relationships between personality and cognition during aging. (a) Neuroticism and inductive reasoning; (b) positive emotions and verbal fluency (data from Graham & Lachman, 2014). These results show very different profiles of cognitive declines with different personality characteristics.

fluency than those who did, whereas older adults who sought out positive emotions had higher verbal fluency than others.

Note, however, that none of the studies on the relationships between personality and cognition have examined age-related differences in strategic variations underlying cognitive performance. And yet, as we have seen throughout this book, the possibility that differences in cognitive performance might be associated to strategy differences should always be taken into account. It would thus be interesting to try and determine whether any differences (or lack thereof) in relationships between personality and cognitive performance during aging are mediated by strategic variations.

If changes with age in the relationships between personality and cognition are mediated by strategic variations, then the way in which personality and cognitive performance are related should itself be connected to age-related differences in strategy repertoire, distribution, execution, and/or selection. For example, Graham and Lachman's (2014) observation that young adults with high neuroticism had better reasoning performance than those with lower neuroticism could be due to the two groups using different reasoning strategies; using the same strategies but in different proportions or with different speed or accuracy; or else selecting different strategies on particular types of items. Insofar as the authors did not examine the type of strategies that participants used on each item, it is impossible to say what role such strategy differences played in the distinct inductive reasoning performance of the two groups of young adults. Similarly, it is impossible to say whether the two groups of older adults with different scores on the neuroticism scale, but similar inductive reasoning performance, used the same strategies. This would be possible if, for example, older adults with a lower score on the neuroticism scale began to use the same strategies as young adults with a higher neuroticism score, and older adults with a high neuroticism score used the same strategies as young adults with a low neuroticism score. In other words, changes with age in the links between personality and cognition, at least in the domain of reasoning, may be associated to (and even mediated by) strategy changes. The same question can be asked (and the same logic used to find the answer) with regard to verbal fluency, whose relationship to positive emotions was reversed in older adults with respect to young adults.

Evidently, in order to answer this type of question, it is not enough to give participants cognitive tests and record their overall performance. Moreover, the strategies they use must be assessed not only overall, but on each item. This involves an enormous amount of additional analyses and observations, but the result is a very large information gain. Using this type of data, we can identify the contexts in which the relationships between personality and cognition change during aging more accurately and more precisely. We can also better characterize the factors, and notably the cognitive factors (i.e., changes in the underlying mechanisms), that determine how the relationships between personality and cognition change with aging.

Aging and relationships between emotions and cognition

Research spanning more than three decades has clearly established that our emotions influence our cognitive performance (see Moore & Oaksford, 2002; Pessoa, 2012, for reviews). The effects of emotions on cognitive performance have been studied using various approaches, including protocols based on inducing emotional states (e.g., viewing videos with strong emotional content, listening to music that is known to trigger emotions), probing the emotions participants recall or feel when certain situations are evoked, examining the cognitive processing of words with emotional content, and questionnaires or interviews about the occurrence and management of emotions. Emotions have been shown to have effects on many cognitive mechanisms, from perceptual–attentional mechanisms (e.g., see Yiend, 2010, for a review) to mechanisms at the highest level, such as inference (e.g., see Blanchette & Richards, 2013, for a review). The results of Niedenthal and Setterlund (1994) offer an illustrative example of the effects of emotions on cognitive performance. They observed that happy participants responded more quickly than sad participants in a lexical decision task (i.e., indicating whether a sequence of letters forms a word or not) to happiness-related words, but not to other positive words. DeSteno, Petty, Wegener, and Rucker (2000) observed that angry participants judged the occurrence of events that are likely to cause anger more probable, whereas sad participants judged saddening events to be more likely.

In the domain of aging, numerous studies have shown that the role of emotions in cognition changes with age (see Carstensen & Mikels, 2005). For example, Mikels, Larkin, Reuter-Lorenz, and Carstensen (2005) tested 20 young participants (between the ages of 18 and 28 years) and 20 older participants (between the ages of 64 and 80 years) on a working-memory task. In each trial, the participants first saw an image on a computer screen for 5 seconds. Next, they saw a fixation cross for 3 seconds, followed by a second image for 5 seconds, and finally a fixation cross once again. The participants were informed that the first image (e.g., a picture of a wolf) might provoke an emotion of variable intensity. They were instructed to maintain this emotion at the same level of intensity while looking at the fixation cross. They then saw a second image (e.g., of a snake) which would also produce an emotion of variable intensity. Finally, when the fixation cross reappeared, they had to indicate whether the emotion they felt when they saw the second image was more or less intense than the one they felt on seeing the first. This was an emotional information retention condition. Mikels et al. compared the performance difference between young and older adults in this condition to the one found in a condition where their participants had to retain visual information. In the latter, participants were asked to remember the brightness intensity of the first image on the computer screen and compare it to the brightness of the second image. The emotions induced by the images could be either negative (e.g., a snake) or positive (e.g., a baby seal).

As the results summarized in Figure 7.6 show, Mikels et al. observed an age-related deficit when older adults' working memory was tested on stimuli that contrasted only in visual terms, whereas there was no effect of age with emotional images. Moreover, while young participants performed better with negatively charged images than with ones that provoke positive emotions, older participants' working memory was better for positively charged images than for negatively charged images. This so-called positivity bias in older adults, or moderating positive effect of emotions in cognitive aging, has been observed in tasks in many other cognitive domains, such as long-term memory, judgment, reasoning, decision making, and tasks assessing attentional mechanisms or judgments of the pleasantness/ unpleasantness of situations or stimuli (e.g., Charles, Mather, & Carstensen, 2003;

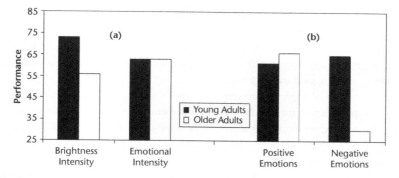

FIGURE 7.6   Young and older participants' performance in a working-memory task with (a) visual information vs. emotional information, and (b) images that provoke positive emotions vs. negative emotions (data from Mikels et al., 2005). These results show an age-related deficit in working memory when participants had to retain visual information, but no deficit when they had to retain emotional information. Moreover, young participants better retained negative emotions and older adults positive emotions.

Mather & Carstensen, 2003, 2005; Rahhal, Hasher, & Colcombe, 2001; Rahhal, May, & Hasher, 2002; Vieillard & Bigand, 2014).

The question then becomes how to explain this positivity bias in older adults, and more generally, how the role of emotions changes during cognitive aging. Carstensen and colleagues (Carstensen, Isaacowitz, & Charles, 1999) proposed the theory of socio-emotional selectivity. According to this theory, cognitive goals and processes are partly determined by temporal contexts. When we perceive time as though it were practically unlimited, as is often the case for young adults, we pay more attention to preparing the future; we invest much more time in accumulating experiences, and in acquiring knowledge and skills. But when we perceive our time as limited (as is the case for older adults, as well as young adults suffering from terminal illness), we focus more on important emotional aspects of our lives, such as the desire to live a meaningful life, and the quality of our social and intimate relationships. According to socio-emotional selectivity theory, this focus makes our emotional processing more efficient. Hence the lack of differences between young and older adults when performing cognitive tasks that require emotional processing.

It seems likely that the accentuated focus on the emotional aspects of life with advancing age is in fact responsible for efficient cognitive-emotional processing and thereby enables older adults, under certain conditions, to counteract the deleterious effects of aging on cognition. But neither the socio-emotional selection theory itself nor the resulting empirical research has really revealed what processing mechanisms participants draw upon when performing emotional and nonemotional tasks. As a result, we do not know, for example, whether older adults' cognitive performance is equivalent to that of young adults on certain emotional tasks because they use the same processes or strategies as young adults (and do so just as efficiently), or whether they succeed in maintaining their cognitive performance using other types of strategies. To find this out, we need to assess, precisely and in detail, how young and older participants perform different tasks. In other words, a strategy approach would allow us to better study how the role of emotions in cognition changes during aging.

The example of regret management strategies illustrates the value of taking a strategy approach to studying how the role of emotions changes during cognitive aging. In a study on regret, Bjälkebring, Västfjäll, and Johansson (2013) sent 108 participants between the ages of 19 and 89 years an email every day for 7 days containing a link to an on-line questionnaire. In addition to questions about their personal characteristics (e.g., age, sex), the participants had to indicate a decision that they had made during the day and categorize it as relating to their finances, work, leisure, consumption, or other. For each decision, they had to say how much they regretted it on a scale from 1 (not at all) to 5 (a lot). For each decision, the participants were asked about the seven regret management strategies defined by Zeelenberg and Pieters (2007). They had to indicate the degree to which they had used each one on a scale from 1 (not at all) to 5 (a lot). These strategies were described as follows: (1) "I try to avoid additional information about the decision." (2) "I will try to redo the decision." (3) "I try to motivate myself to think that the decision was right." (4) "The outcome of the decision was not my fault." (5) "I will try to change to another alternative." (6) "I try to reevaluate the decision." (7) "I try not to think about it." Moreover, the participants had to indicate a future decision that they had thought about over the previous 24 hours, and that they had not yet taken. They also had to indicate (on a scale from 1 to 5) to what extent they had used the six regret prevention strategies proposed by Zeelenberg and Pieters (2007): (1) "I try to get additional information before making the decision." (2) "I try to be totally sure the decision is right before making it." (3) "I try to get support from someone else." (4) "I try to delay the decision." (5) "I try to make sure I can change to another alternative." (6) "I expect to feel regret."

When Bjälkebring, Västfjäll, and Johansson (2013) examined the distribution of regretted decisions, it emerged that the percentages of regretted decisions and decisions where participants anticipated possible regret differed with age. For example, 45% of young adults' decisions led to regret (vs. 20% of those of older adults). Moreover, older adults were less likely to anticipate regretting a decision (60%) than young adults (90%). More generally, Bjälkebring et al. found a negative correlation between participants' age and the number of decisions that led to regret ($r = -0.24$), first, and the number of anticipated regrets ($r = -0.36$), second. They also found that some strategies were more effective at preventing regret than others (i.e., the number of times subjects used them was negatively correlated with regrets following decisions). This was true, for example, of the following strategies: (1) "I try to be totally sure the decision is right before making it." (2) "I try to delay the decision." (3) "I expect to feel regret." More interestingly, the efficacy of regret prevention strategies varied with age. The decision reevaluation strategy led to decreased regret in older adults but increased regret in young adults. The authors even found that the use of this strategy was an effective mediator of changes in regret management during aging.

This example illustrates how the strategy approach can be used to understand how the role of emotions in cognition changes as we age, both conceptually (by providing information on the types of processes involved at different ages in adulthood) and methodologically (by helping to establish valid and reliable methods for assessing the strategies used, as well as their efficacy). The strategy approach could be just as informative in assessing the links between emotion and cognition over the lifecourse in numerous other cognitive domains as it is in decision making. It should allow us to explain many effects seen in older adults' processing of emotional information. To take just one recent example, Vieillard and Bigand (2014) found that listening to menacing pieces of music generated less intense emotions in older adults than in young adults, but that joyful music led to stronger preferences in older adults than in young adults (see also Vieillard, Didierjean, & Maquestiaux, 2012). These judgments likely result from differences in music-processing strategies between young and older adults, but this could be established empirically by directly examining these strategies.

Pathological aging and strategy variations

A commonality between the various pathologies associated to aging (dementia, depression, stroke, etc.) is that they lead to major, and sometimes progressive, cognitive disturbances (see Dujardin & Lemaire, 2008, and Ravdin & Katzen, 2013, for overviews). The strategy perspective, which has been defended throughout this book as a way of characterizing and understanding cognitive aging, could also be more systematically applied in pathological aging than it currently is. Its value in this context can be illustrated with reference to a particular form of dementia, dementia of Alzheimer type. Not only is Alzheimer's the most frequent type of dementia, but a number of studies examining strategic variations in AD patients have already been performed. Before discussing a few interesting results from this literature, I will briefly present the diagnostic criteria for this disease, as well as a few illustrations of the cognitive deficits that it produces.

The American Psychiatric Association has established the following diagnostic criteria for AD:

a. The development of multiple cognitive deficits manifested by both memory impairment (impaired ability to learn new information or to recall previously learned information) as well as one (or more) of the following cognitive disturbances: Aphasia (language disturbances), apraxia (impaired ability to carry out motor activities despite intact motor function), agnosia (failure to recognize or identify objects despite intact sensory function), disturbance in executive functioning (i.e., planning, organizing, sequencing, abstracting).

b. These cognitive deficits each cause significant impairment in social or occupational functioning and represent a significant decline from a previous level of functioning.

c.   The course is characterized by gradual onset and continuing cognitive decline.
d.   These cognitive deficits are not due to other central nervous system conditions (e.g., cerebrovascular disease), systemic conditions that are known to cause dementia (e.g., hypothyroidism), or substance-induced conditions.
e.   The deficits do not occur exclusively during the course of a delirium.
f.   The disturbance is not better accounted for by another disorder (e.g., major depressive disorder).

These criteria are important both in defining the disease and in clinical practice. However, because of their high level of generality, they do not suffice to exhaustively specify the various cognitive manifestations of AD. This is true both at the general level (e.g., are the affected mechanisms specific to certain cognitive activities, such as episodic memory, or do they also affect other activities in similar proportions, such as reasoning and language?) and in more specific terms (e.g., Is the decline in memory encoding as large as the decline in retrieval processes?). The numerous studies carried out from a cognitive perspective (see Collette, Feyers, & Bastin, 2008, and Pena-Casanova, Sanchez-Benavides, de Sola, Manero-Borras, & Casals-Coll, 2012, for reviews) have offered some responses to these types of questions.

AD is known to affect short-term memory and various long-term memory functions (episodic memory, procedural and implicit memory, autobiographical memory, metamemory), as well as attentional and executive systems, language, and semantic processes. The proportional distribution of these effects depends on the level of advancement of the disease. For example, in short-term memory, recency effects (i.e., better performance on the final items in a list to be learned) are reduced in Alzheimer's patients, suggesting a deficit in short-term storage, whereas information maintenance mechanisms are apparently not, or less, affected, as suggested by the equivalence of phonological similarity effects (i.e., better recall for phonologically different words than for phonologically similar words) in AD patients and older adult controls. Another example is in long-term memory, where Alzheimer's patients show smaller priming effects (i.e., improved performance on an item following exposure to the same item or an item that is similar semantically, emotionally, phonologically) than older control participants on production tasks (e.g., completing a word fragment), but equivalent priming effects on identification tasks (i.e., where they have to say what is shown in an intact or degraded image of an object). Disturbances (combined with preservations) of procedural learning abilities (assessed with pursuit tasks, mirror tracing, puzzles, weight judgments, etc.) have been observed.

In another example, Piolino et al. (2003) found that the decline in AD patients' autobiographical memory affects episodic memories (i.e., memories that can be situated in a precise spatiotemporal context) more than semantic memories (i.e., recall for generic events without memory for context). And selective attention mechanisms, particularly inhibition mechanisms, deteriorate as a result of the disease, as attested by the greater Stroop interference effects (and weaker negative priming effects) observed in AD patients than in older adult controls. Some researchers (e.g., Amieva, Phillips, Della Sala, & Henry, 2004) have proposed an interesting distinction between the inhibition mechanisms that are most affected in AD, as seen in tasks requiring voluntary inhibition (e.g., Stroop effects), and mechanisms involving more automatic inhibition (e.g., inhibition of return), the latter being more affected during aging. In the domain of language, research has demonstrated numerous deficits in both production (e.g., more tip-of-the-tongue words than in healthy older adult controls) and comprehension (and in particular the comprehension of complex sentences, which, because it requires inference, is more difficult for patients). These deficits worsen with the advancement of the disease. Research on AD has thus shown that the disease has distinct effects on performance in different domains of cognition. These depend, of course, on the advancement of the disease; but, most importantly for our purposes, they also depend on the cognitive domain studied, and within a given domain, the task used.

Studies that have sought to map out the cognitive activities and tasks that are either affected or preserved in pathological aging have led to major progress in our knowledge of the cognitive manifestations of the disease. One of the limitations of such studies, however, is that it is often difficult to determine how patients perform the cognitive tasks that they are given, and consequently whether the disease changes how they try and do so. Finding this out is one of the objectives of the strategy approach. A few studies have already been conducted along these lines. Some have shown that older control participants and AD patients use the same strategies in some cognitive domains and/or certain tasks, but use these strategies in different proportions. Other studies have found—sometimes in the same domains (but with different tasks), sometimes in different domains—that the two groups of participants differed both in their use and their execution of strategies.

For example, Arnaud, Lemaire, Allen, and Michel (2008) tested 40 young participants, 40 healthy older participants, and 23 patients in the early stages of AD. Our participants had to solve 40 simple subtractions: 20 easier problems (e.g., 7 − 3) and 20 harder problems (e.g., 12 − 7). The older controls and the patients were matched on their level of education and age (between ages 60 and 80). All the participants were tested in choice and no-choice conditions. In the choice condition, they could choose to use either a retrieval strategy or some other strategy on each problem. When using retrieval strategies, they could, for example, directly retrieve the result from memory (e.g., they had previously memorized that 12 − 8 = 4) or use addition (e.g., they knew that 6 + 3 = 9, hence 9 − 6 = 3). All other strategies were classified as "nonretrieval" strategies: These included counting (e.g., solving 9 − 3 by calculating 9 − 1 − 1 − 1 or 6 + 1 + 1 + 1), decomposition (e.g., solving 11 − 4 as 11 − 2 − 2 = 7), and other strategies (e.g., the participants were unable to verbalize their strategies and just said "I just counted"). In the choice condition, we asked each participant after each problem "Did you use a retrieval or a nonretrieval strategy?" Before doing so, we had made sure that all the participants understood what a retrieval strategy was and what the other strategies were. We also performed a series of statistical analyses to test the validity of our verbal protocols and to determine whether the participants, including AD patients, in fact reported using a retrieval strategy when they had retrieved the answer and another strategy when they had not done so, and whether the strategy participants said they had used was the one they had actually implemented. In the no-choice condition, the participants had to solve exactly the same problems, this time attempting to use the retrieval strategy on all problems. The data from the choice condition allowed us to analyze the strategies participants used (in other words, how participants chose to perform the task), and the data from the no-choice condition allowed us to determine whether the efficacy of the retrieval strategy differed between the groups and/or depending on the difficulty of the problems. The results showed that the pathology had no effects on strategy use or selection, but significantly affected strategy execution.

Healthy older control participants used the retrieval strategy to solve 75% of the harder problems and 91% of the easy problems (the corresponding percentages in AD patients were 80% and 95%). There were no statistically significant differences between the groups. As the results in Figure 7.7 clearly show, however, the patients' performance was considerably slower than that of healthy older controls, particularly on harder problems. The results on percentages of errors showed a similar pattern. In summary, healthy older control participants and AD patients performed this mental calculation task using the same strategies about the same proportions of the time, but their execution of those strategies differed widely.

Other studies have found that older controls and AD patients differ in both strategy use and execution. For example, in a study on numerosity estimation abilities, Gandini, Lemaire, and Michel (2009) also used the choice/no-choice method to compare the strategy use and execution of healthy older controls and AD patients.

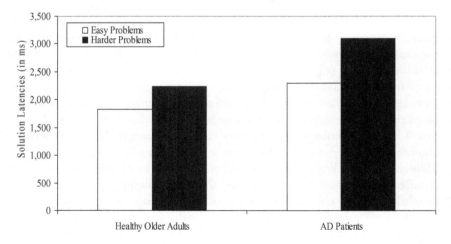

FIGURE 7.7 Solution times for easier and harder subtraction problems in older adult controls and Alzheimer's disease (AD) patients (data from Arnaud et al., 2008). These results show that patients' performance was slower than that of controls, especially on harder problems.

The participants saw collections of dots on a computer screen and had to estimate their approximate number. Small collections included between 20 and 39 dots, and large collections between 40 and 65 dots. On the basis of previous studies establishing the repertoire of strategies spontaneously used by young and older participants (Gandini, Lemaire, & Dufau, 2008), in the choice condition we asked the participants to choose between using the perceptual estimation strategy and the anchoring (or approximate counting) strategy to estimate the numerosity of each collection. All the participants were then tested in two no choice conditions, one where they had to use the perceptual estimation strategy on each collection, and another where they had to systematically apply the anchoring strategy.

In the choice condition, AD patients more often used the perceptual estimation strategy (and thus less often the anchoring strategy) than healthy older controls, which is consistent with the hypothesis that participants in the two groups would perform the numerosity estimation task in somewhat different ways. More interestingly still, strategy selection varied significantly more with the numerosity of the collection in patients than in healthy older controls. The patients used the perceptual estimation strategy on 71% of small collections and on 80% of large collections (the corresponding percentages in older controls were 64% and 69%). It is as if, at least in its early stages, AD did not decrease the efficacy of patients' abilities to adapt their strategy choices to the characteristics of the problems, although the two groups' strategy preferences differed overall.

The results on strategy performance from the no-choice condition revealed different Strategy × Numerosity interactions in healthy older controls and AD patients (Figure 7.8). Older controls were slower at estimating the numerosity of the large collections than that of the small collections using both strategies; this performance difference was larger with the anchoring strategy than with the perceptual estimation strategy. AD patients took the same amount of time to estimate the size of small and large collections when executing the perceptual estimation strategy, but more time to execute the anchoring strategy on large collections than on small ones.

As in the case of normal aging, a strategy perspective can enrich our understanding of the impact of pathology on cognitive performance both at a global level (i.e., do AD patients and healthy age-matched controls use the same strategies to perform cognitive tasks?) and on a more specific level (i.e., does this or that factor have a greater impact on patients' cognitive performance than on that of age-matched controls?). Two examples illustrate the specific level of analysis: One concerns strategy selection (inter-item strategy repetition effects), the other strategy execution (sequential difficulty effects).

Lemaire and Leclère (2014b) demonstrated an influence of AD on inter-item strategy repetitions, a specific effect on strategy selection. We asked 30 healthy older control participants and 30 early-stage AD patients to perform a computational estimation task on two-digit multiplication problems. The participants were instructed to choose the best of two possible strategies on each problem, rounding-down (i.e., using 40 × 70 to estimate 42 × 76) or rounding-up (i.e., using 50 × 80). The participants underwent 48 trials, each composed of three successive problems. The problems were carefully selected such that the best strategy on the

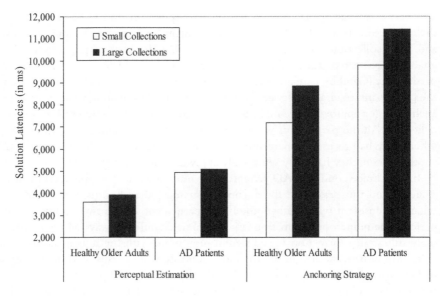

FIGURE 7.8 Solution latencies of Alzheimer's disease (AD) patients and healthy older control participants on a numerosity estimation task with small and large collections of dots using perceptual estimation and anchoring strategies in the no-choice condition (data from Gandini et al., 2009). These results show that the patients were slower than age-matched controls, particularly on more difficult problems and with the most cognitively demanding strategy (i.e., anchoring).

first and third problems was rounding-down (e.g., 61 × 32) on half the trials and rounding-up (e.g., 89 × 68) on the other trials. On every trial, the second problem was neutral (e.g., 47 × 63) and choosing the best strategy was difficult because the unit digits were not salient cues and used to select the best strategy. The question was whether or not the older controls and the AD patients would show an equally strong tendency to repeat the strategy used on the first problem. In another study (Lemaire & Leclère, 2014a), we had found that older adults have a greater tendency to repeat the same strategy than young adults. The results of this study with AD patients revealed that they tended to do so even more often than age-matched controls. For example, on items where the better strategy on the second problem was different than the one on the first problem (i.e., where the participants should not have repeated their strategy), older controls repeated the same strategy in 39% of cases, whereas AD patients repeated their strategy in 71% of cases. In other words, strategy repetitions on two successive problems were considerably more frequent in AD patients than in age-matched controls. This phenomenon, which could be seen as a form of strategy perseverance, seems to result in part from executive deficits which occur beginning very early in the course of the disease. This deficit apparently causes AD patients to have more difficulty than age-matched controls in disengaging from the strategy that they have just executed in order to initiate a new strategy which is better adapted to the problem that they currently face.

Uittenhove and Lemaire (2012, 2013a, b) demonstrated the influence of AD on the strategy sequential difficulty effect, which is specific to strategy execution. In this effect, the execution time of a strategy on a given problem varies depending on whether the previous problem was solved using an easier or a more difficult strategy. Both young and older participants generally execute a strategy more slowly when they executed a more difficult strategy on the previous trial. Uittenhove and Lemaire (2013b) tested 25 older controls and 41 patients in the early stages of AD (mean Mini-Mental State Examination score = 19.6). The participants performed a computational estimation task on the products of pairs of two-digit numbers, such as 32 × 67. On the target problems, they had to use the mixed-rounding strategy (i.e., in this case, 30 × 70). Half of the target problems were preceded by a problem that the participants had to estimate using a more difficult strategy (i.e., here, rounding the two operands up to the nearest decade and using 40 × 70); the other half were preceded by problems that the participants had to estimate with an easier strategy (i.e., here, rounding the two operands down to the nearest decade, using 30 × 60). The results showed that strategy sequential difficulty effect (i.e., the difference in solution times between problems following so-called hard problems and problems following so-called easy problems) was almost nine times larger in AD patients than in age-matched controls. Older controls took 3,931 ms and 3,751 ms (a significant difference of 180 ms) to execute the mixed-rounding strategy following problems estimated using a harder strategy and an easier strategy respectively. The corresponding times in AD patients were 9,299 ms and 7,708 ms (a difference of 1,591 ms), respectively. In other words, the sequence in which strategies were executed had a much larger influence in patients than in healthy age-matched controls. As this effect results in part from a decrease in processing resources (which are monopolized by the execution of the strategy used to solve the previous problem) and from slowness in reinitializing the system to solve a new problem, this Sequential Difficulty × Group interaction reveals that these processes are very strongly affected starting from the onset of AD.

These studies (Arnaud et al., 2008; Gandini et al., 2009; Uittenhove & Lemaire, 2013b) were conducted in the domain of arithmetic problem solving. But there is no reason to think that the strategic variations associated to AD (or to another neurodegenerative disease) are restricted to this cognitive domain. In all of the domains where strategic variations have already been studied (as well as in domains where it would be straightforward to study them either using direct or indirect methods), it should be possible to take the strategy perspective. Studying the strategic variations associated to AD (or any other pathology of aging) promises to deepen our understanding of what processes are affected by the disease, when they are affected, and in what proportions. This systematic study would also allow us to identify the tasks where strategy variations are (or are not) influenced by dementia, and those where the disease does not affect patients' strategy execution.

The strategy perspective allows us to do more than simply observe that a cognitive deficit is present. It allows us to better characterize it, specifying its nature, the conditions of its occurrence, and the underlying mechanisms.

General conclusions

Whether in the study of the effects of cognitive training, how the links between cognition and personality or emotions change with age, or pathological aging, the findings mentioned in this chapter illustrate the value of a strategy approach in understanding cognitive aging. These results reinforce the idea that achieving a deeper understanding of these questions depends on examining the strategies that we use to perform cognitive tasks and how those strategies change as we age, under the influence of training, personality, emotions, and pathology. The strategy approach can also be extended to many domains not covered in this book and where previous research has demonstrated significant change during aging. For example, it would be interesting to see what contributions the strategy approach can make to our understanding of the role played by our physical condition, lifestyle, and profession in cognitive change as we age. Moreover, as I have pointed out a number of times in the course of the book, there is no reason to limit this approach to the domain of cognition. It can be just as fruitfully used, for example, to understand changes with age in our social relationships (i.e., how our career objectives and our relationships to our colleagues change over time) or our personal relationships (i.e., how the types of friendships we have change as we go through life). Future studies in these domains which adopt a strategy perspective will enable us to arrive at more complete empirical answers than those that are currently available. This will be possible because taking the strategy perspective allows us not only to ask the "classical" questions about aging (e.g., What declines/remains stable in older people?), but also to address new and different issues. The strategy perspective pushes us to ask questions such as: What approaches do young and older people take to accomplishing a given task? What distinguishes the approach that successfully aging individuals take to a task from the approaches adopted by other, less successfully aging individuals? It should, of course, help us find answers to these questions at both the behavioral and neural levels.

Future studies will also examine questions about strategic variations during aging whose currently available answers are not entirely satisfactory. For example, we currently do not know what characterizes the situations or domains where the strategies participants use (types of strategies, as well as percentages of use of each strategy) either do or do not influence aging-related performance differences. In this book we have seen many examples of cases where performance differences between young and older adults are systematically associated to strategy differences. In other cases, however, strategy variations do not play a determinant role in age-related performance differences. This double pattern (which is sometimes found within a single domain, or even a single task) does not take away from the value of a strategy approach. On the contrary, in cases where strategy variations are associated to performance differences during aging, it means that these strategy variations contribute to change in cognitive performance with aging. This is observed, notably, when older participants perform less well than younger participants because they use less efficacious strategies; because they use efficacious strategies on far fewer items; or when they use generally efficacious strategies as often as young people, but are unable to select them as systematically to respond specifically to items where they lead to better performance. In other words, these are cases where performance variations can at least partly be explained by differences in the mechanisms recruited by young and older participants. In other cases, in contrast, age-related strategy variations are not correlated with performance differences, as when young and older participants use different strategies but achieve similar performance, or use the same strategies but perform at different levels. In cases where older adults perform as well as young adults while using different strategies, the use of these different strategies likely enables older adults to compensate for what otherwise would be performance deficits. This is one of the multiple forms of functional compensation available to the aging brain. In cases where identical strategies are associated to different performance levels, it is likely that aging leads to deterioration in the execution of strategies, or even simply in their initiation (i.e., taking more time to begin executing a strategy is enough to lead to longer latencies). In any case, the strategy approach has the merit of improving our understanding of how older participants perform the tasks that we give them. This puts us in a better position to characterize the different ways of thinking at each step in adult life.

Another important question about aging-related strategy variations that future studies will shed light on concerns the determinants of strategy variations during aging. What leads older adults, in some cases, to use strategies that are simpler but less efficacious than those chosen by young adults, or to use the same strategies but to be less able to execute them accurately and quickly, even in domains where they have greater expertise than young adults (e.g., mental calculation)? And what, in other cases, prevents older adults from systematically choosing the best strategy on each item, even when they are as aware of what it is as young adults are? As I have mentioned several times in this book, the decrease in our processing resources with age, which results partly from physiological deterioration (e.g., decreases in brain volume, interregional connectivity, dopaminergic deficits; see Raz, 2000, and Cabeza et al., 2005, for reviews), seems to bear a great deal of the responsibility. We have seen that, in some domains and on some tasks, cognitive slowing leads older participants to choose the best strategy less often than young participants do. We have also seen that the decline of certain executive functions (such as inhibition and flexibility) is sometimes responsible for the decrease in the number of strategies that older adults use on a task. It is a safe bet that future studies will attempt to distinguish between the contributions of general mechanisms (such as processing resources) and more specific ones (like expertise in a domain) to age-related strategic variations. It is also a safe bet that advances in our understanding of how the brain basis of cognition changes with age will allow us to better understand how, as the aging brain attempts to optimize the adaptation of brain resources to cognitive task demands, it is led to modify strategy parameters in order to perform different tasks (Cabeza et al., 2005; Cabeza & Dennis, 2012).

In sum, because the strategy perspective is extremely fruitful, its adoption in future studies will enable us to make major progress in our understanding of the fundamental mechanisms of cognitive aging. This progress can be expected to relate both to empirical phenomena (revealing the behavioral and neural manifestations of aging) and the theoretical level (in computational models of how the cognitive system ages). This progress will likely not be limited to the domain of cognition, but will extend to other domains of mental life.

REFERENCES

Adams, C. (1991). Qualitative age differences in memory for text: A life-span developmental perspective. *Psychology and Aging, 6*, 323–336.

Aiken-Morgan, A. T., Bichsel, J., Allaire, J. C., Savla, J., Edwards, C. L., & Whitfield, K. E. (2012). Personality as a source of individual differences in cognitive aging among African American older adults. *Journal of Research in Personality, 46*, 465–471.

Allen, P. A., Ashcraft, M. H., & Weber, T. A. (1992). On mental multiplication and age. *Psychology and Aging, 7*, 536–545.

Allen, P. A., Bucur, B., Grabbe, J., Work, T., & Madden, D. J. (2011). Influence of encoding difficulty, word frequency, and phonological regularity on age differences in word naming. *Experimental Aging Research, 37*(3), 261–292.

Allen, P. A., Bucur, B., Lemaire, P., Duverne, S., Ogrocki, P., & Sanders, R. E. (2005). Influence of probable Alzheimer's disease on multiplication verification and production. *Aging, Neuropsychology, and Cognition, 12*, 1–31.

Allen, P. A., Smith, A. F., Jerge, K. A., & Vires-Collins, H. (1997). Age differences in mental multiplication: Evidence for peripheral but not central decrements. *Journal of Gerontology: Psychological Sciences, 52b*(2), 81–90.

Amieva, H., Phillips, L. H., Della Sala, S., & Henry, J. D. (2004). Inhibitory functioning in Alzheimer's disease: A review. *Brain, 127*, 949–964.

Ardiale, E., & Lemaire, P. (2012). Age-related differences in within-item strategy switching. *Psychology and Aging, 27*, 1138–1151.

Ardiale, E., & Lemaire, P. (2013). Effects of execution duration on within-item strategy switching in young and older adults. *Journal of Cognitive Psychology. 25*(4), 464–472.

Ardiale, E., Hodzik, S., & Lemaire, P. (2012). Aging and strategy switch costs: A study in arithmetic problem solving. *L'Année Psychologique, 112*, 345–360.

Arenberg, D. (1982). Changes with age in problem solving. In F. I. M. Craik & S. Trehub (Eds.), *Aging and cognitive processes*. New York: Plenum.

Arnaud, L., Lemaire, P., Allen, P., & Michel, B.-F. (2008). Strategic aspects of young, healthy older adults', and Alzheimer patients' arithmetic performance. *Cortex, 44*, 119–130.

Arning, K., & Ziefle, M. (2009). Effects of age, cognitive, and personal factors on PDA menu navigation performance. *Behaviour and Information Technology, 28*(3), 251–268.

Ashcraft, M. H., & Battaglia, J. (1978). Evidence for retrieval and decision processes in mental addition. *Journal of Experimental Psychology: Human Learning and Memory, 4*, 527–538.

Ashcraft, M. H., & Stazyk, E. H. (1981). Mental addition: A test of three verification models. *Memory and Cognition, 9*(2), 185–196.

Baker, T. J., & Bichsel, J. (2006). Personality predictors of intelligence: Differences between young and cognitively healthy older adults. *Personality and Individual Differences, 41*, 861–871.

Baltes, P., & Lindenberger, U. (1997). Emergence of a powerful connection between sensory and cognitive functions across the adult lifespan: A new window to the study of cognitive aging. *Psychology and Aging, 12*, 12–21.

Barbeau, E. J., Félician, O., Joubert, S., Sontheimer, A., Ceccaldi, M., & Poncet, M. (2005). Preserved visual recognition memory in an amnesic patient with hippocampal lesions. *Hippocampus, 15*(5), 587–296.

Barbeau, E. J., Pariente, J., Felician, O., & Puel, M. (2011). Visual recognition memory: A double anatomo-functional dissociation. *Hippocampus, 21*(9), 929–934.

Barulli, D. J., Rakitin, B. C., Lemaire P, & Stern, Y. (2013). The influence of cognitive reserve on strategy selection in normal aging. *Journal of the International Neuropsychological Society, 19*(7), 841–844.

Basak, C., & Verhaeghen, P. (2003). Subitizing speed, subitizing range, counting speed, the Stroop effect, and aging: Capacity differences and speed equivalence. *Psychology and Aging, 18*(2), 240–249.

Basak, C., Boot, W. R., Voss, M. W., & Kramer, A. F. (2008). Can training in a real-time strategy video game attenuate cognitive decline in older adults? *Psychology and Aging, 23*(4), 765–777.

Beitz, K. M., Salthouse, T. A., & Davis, H. P. (2014). Performance on the Iowa Gambling Task: From 5 to 89 years of age. *Journal of Experimental Psychology: General, 143*(4), 1677–1689.

Belleville, S., Clement, F., Mellah, S., Gilbert, B., Fontaine, F., & Gauthier, S. (2011). Training-related brain plasticity in subjects at risk of developing Alzheimer's disease. *Brain, 134*(6), 1623–1634.

Bennett, S. J., Elliott, D., & Rodacki, A. (2012). Movement strategies in vertical aiming of older adults. *Experimental Brain Research, 216*(3), 445–455.

Besedes, T., Deck, C., Sarangi, S., & Shor, M. (2012). Age effects and heuristics in decision making. *The Review of Economics and Statistics, 94*(2), 580–595.

Bherer, L., & Belleville, S. (2004a). Age-related differences in response preparation: The role of time uncertainty. *Journal of Gerontology: Psychological Sciences, 59*, 66–74.

Bherer, L., & Belleville, S. (2004b). The effect of training on preparatory attention in older adults: Evidence for the role of uncertainty in age-related preparatory deficits. *Aging, Neuropsychology, and Cognition, 11*(1), 37–50.

Bherer, L., Erickson, K., & Liu-Ambrose, T. (2013). Physical exercise and brain functions in older adults. *Journal of Aging Research*, doi: 10.1155/2013/657508.

Bjälkebring, P., Västfjäll, D., & Johansson, B. (2013). Regulation of experienced and anticipated regret for daily decisions in younger and older adults in a Swedish one-week diary study. *GeroPsych, 26*(4), 233–241.

Blanchette, I. & Richards, A. (2013). Is emotional Stroop interference linked to affective responses? Evidence from skin conductance and facial electromyography. *Emotion, 13*, 129–138.

Booth, J., Schinka, J., Brown, L., Mortimer, J. A., & Borenstein, A. R. (2006). Five-factor personality dimensions, mood states, and cognitive performance in older adults. *Journal of Clinical and Experimental Neuropsychology, 28*, 676–683.

Bouazzaoui, B., Isingrini, M., Fay, S., Angel, L., Vanneste, S., Clarys, D., & Taconnat, L. (2010). Aging, executive functioning and self-reported memory strategy use. *Acta Psychologica, 135*, 59–66.

Boucard, G. K., Albinet, C. T., Bugaiska, A., Bouquet, C. A., Clarys, D., & Audiffren, M. (2012). Impact of physical activity on executive functions in aging: A selective effect on inhibition among old adults. *Journal of Sport and Exercise Psychology, 34*, 808–827.

Boyke, J., Driemeyer, J., Gaser, C., Büchel, C., & May, A. (2008). Training induced brain structure changes in the elderly. *Journal of Neuroscience, 28*, 7031–7035.

Brehmer, Y., Rieckmann, A., Bellander, M., Westerberg, H., Fischer, H., & Bäckman, L. (2011). Neural correlates of training-related working memory gains in old age. *NeuroImage, 58*, 1110–1120.

Brom, S., & Kliegel, M. (2014). Improving everyday prospective memory performance in older adults: Comparing cognitive process and strategy training. *Psychology and Aging, 29*, 744–755.

Bruyer, R., Van der Linden, M., Rectem, D., & Galvez, C. (1995). Effects of age and education in the Stroop interference. *Archives de Psychologie, 63*, 257–267.

Bugaiska, A., Clarys, D., Jarry, C., Taconnat, L., Tapia, G., Vanneste, S., & Isingrini. M. (2007). The effect of aging in recollective experience: The processing speed and executive functioning hypothesis. *Consciousness and Cognition, 16*(4), 797–808.

Buitenweg, J. I., Murre, J. M., & Ridderikhof, K. R. (2012). Brain training in progress: A review of trainability in healthy seniors. *Frontiers in Human Neuroscience, 6*, 183.

Buschkuehl, M., Jaeggi, S. M., Hutchison, S., & Perrig-Chiello, P. (2008). Impact of working memory training on memory performance in old-old adults. *Psychology and Aging, 23*(4), 743–753.

Cabeza, R., & Dennis, N.A. (2012). Frontal lobes and aging: Deterioration and compensation. In D. T. Stuss & R. T. Knight (Eds.), *Principles of frontal lobe function* (2nd ed., pp. 628–652). New York: Oxford University Press.

Cabeza, R., Nyberg, L. L., & Park, D. C. (2005). *Cognitive neuroscience of aging: Linking cognitive and cerebral aging.* Oxford: Oxford University Press.

Carstensen, L. L., Isaacowitz, D., & Charles, S. T. (1999). Taking time seriously: A theory of socioemotional selectivity. *American Psychologist, 54*, 165–181.

Carstensen, L. L., & Mikels, J.A. (2005). At the intersection of emotion and cognition: Aging and the positivity effect. *Current Directions in Psychological Science, 14*, 117–121.

Carstensen, L. L., & Turk-Charles, S. (1994). The salience of emotion across the adult life span. *Psychology and Aging, 9*, 259–264.

Castel, A. D. (2005). Memory for grocery prices in younger and older adults: The role of schematic support. *Psychology and Aging, 20*, 718–721.

Castel, A. D. (2008). The adaptive and strategic use of memory by older adults: Evaluative processing and value-directed remembering. In A. S. Benjamin & B. H. Ross (Eds.), *The psychology of learning and motivation* (Vol. 48, pp. 225–270). London, England: Academic Press.

Castel, A. D., Balota, D. A., & McCabe, D. P. (2009). Memory efficiency and the strategic control of attention at encoding: Impairments of value-directed remembering in Alzheimer's disease. *Neuropsychology, 23*, 297–306.

Castel, A. D., Benjamin, A. S., Craik, F. I. M., & Watkins, M. J. (2002). The effects of aging on selectivity and control in short-term recall. *Memory and Cognition, 30*, 1078–1085.

Castel, A. D., Farb, N., & Craik, F. I. M. (2007). Memory for general and specific value information in younger and older adults: Measuring the limits of strategic control. *Memory and Cognition, 35*, 689–700.

Castel, A. D., Humphreys, K. L., Lee, S. S., Galvan, A., Balota, D. A., & McCabe, D. P. (2011). The development of memory efficiency and value-directed remembering across the life span: A cross-sectional study of memory and selectivity. *Developmental Psychology,* 47(6), 1553–1564.

Castel, A. D., McGillivray, S., & Friedman, M. C. (2012). Metamemory and memory efficiency in older adults: Learning about the benefits of priority processing and value-directed remembering. In M. Naveh-Benjamin & N. Ohta (Eds.), *Memory and aging: Current issues and future directions* (pp. 245–270). New York: Psychology Press.

Cerella, J. (1985). Information processing rates in the elderly. *Psychological Bulletin, 98,* 67–83.

Chamorro-Premuzic, T., & Furnham, A. (2003a). Personality predicts academic performance: Evidence from two longitudinal university samples. *Journal of Research in Personality, 37*(4), 319–338.

Chamorro-Premuzic, T., & Furnham, A. (2003b). Personality predicts academic performance: Evidence from two longitudinal university samples. *Journal of Research in Personality, 17,* 237–250.

Chamorro-Premuzic, T., & Furnham, A. (2003c). Personality traits and academic examination performance. *European Journal of Personality, 17,* 237–250.

Charles, S. T., Mather, M., & Carstensen, L. L. (2003). Focusing on the positive: Age differences in memory for positive, negative, and neutral stimuli. *Journal of Experimental Psychology: General, 85,* 163–178.

Charness, N., & Campbell, J. I. D. (1988). Acquiring skill at mental calculation in adulthood: A task decomposition. *Journal of Experimental Psychology: General, 117,* 115–129.

Chauvel, G., Maquestiaux, F., Hartley, A. A., Joubert, S., Didierjean, A., & Masters, R. (2012). Age effects shrink when motor learning is predominantly supported by nondeclarative, automatic memory processes: Evidence from golf putting. *Quarterly Journal of Experimental Psychology, 65,* 25–38.

Chen, Y., & Sun, Y. (2003). Age differences in financial decision-making: Using simple heuristics. *Educational Gerontology, 29,* 627–635.

Clark, H. H., & Chase, W. G. (1972). On the process of comparing sentences against pictures. *Cognitive Psychology, 3,* 472–517.

Clarys, D., Isingrini, M., & Gana, K. (2002a). Mediators of age-related differences in recollective experience in recognition memory. *Acta Psychologica, 109,* 315–329.

Clarys, D., Isingrini, M., & Gana, K. (2002b). Aging and episodic memory: Mediators of age differences in remembering and knowing. *Acta Psychologica, 109*(3), 315–329.

Clarys, D., Isingrini, M., & Haerty, A. (2000). Effects of attentional load and ageing on word-stem and word-fragment implicit memory tasks. *European Journal of Cognitive Psychology, 12*(3), 395–412.

Cohen, G., & Faulkner, D. (1983). Age differences in performance on two information-processing tasks: Strategy selection and processing efficiency. *Journal of Gerontology, 38,* 447–454.

Cohen, G., & Faulkner, D. (1986). Memory for proper names: Age differences in retrieval. *British Journal of Developmental Psychology, 4,* 187–197.

Collette, F., Feyers, D., & Bastin, C. (2008). La maladie d'Alzheimer. In K. Dujardin & P. Lemaire (Eds.), *Neuropsychologie du vieillissement normal et pathologique* (pp. 105–122). Paris: Masson.

Cooper, J. A., Worthy, D. A., Gorlick, M. A., & Maddox, W. T. (2013). Scaffolding across the lifespan in history-dependent decision making. *Psychology and Aging, 28*(2), 505–514.

Corr, P. J., & Matthews, G. (2009). *The Cambridge handbook of personality psychology.* Cambridge: Cambridge University Press.

Costa, P. T. Jr., & McRae, R. R. (1992). *Revised NEO Personality Inventory (NEO-PI-R) and NEO Five-Factor Inventory (NEO-FFI) professional manual.* Odessa, FL: Psychological Assessment Resources.

Costello, C., Ovando, D., Hilborn, R., Gaines, S. D., Deschenes, O., & Lester, S. E. (2012). Status and solutions for the world's unassessed fisheries. *Science, 338*, 517–520.

Craik, F. I. M. (2002). Levels of processing: Past, present, and future? *Memory, 10*, 305–318.

Craik, F. I. M., & Salthouse, T. A. (Eds.) (2008). *Handbook of aging and cognition* (3rd ed.). New York: Psychology Press.

Curtis, R., Windsor, T. D., & Soubelet, A. (2014). The relationships between Big-5 personality traits and cognitive ability in older adults – a review. *Aging, Neuropsychology and Cognition, 22*, 42–71

Dahlin, E., Nyberg, L., Bäckman, L., & Stigsdotter Neely, A. (2008). Plasticity of executive functioning in young and older adults: Immediate training gains, transfer, and long-term maintenance. *Psychology and Aging, 23*(4), 720–730.

Davis, H. P., Cohen, A., Gandy, M., Colombo, P., VanDusseldrop, G., Simolke, N., et al. (1990). Lexical priming deficits as a function of age. *Behavioral Neuroscience, 104*(2), 288–297.

Davis, S. W., Dennis, N. A., Daselaar, S. M., Fleck, M. S., & Cabeza, R. (2008). Que PASA? The posterior–anterior shift in aging. *Cerebral Cortex, 18*(5), 1201–1209.

De Rammelaere, S., Stuyven, E., & Vandierendonck, A. (2001). Verifying simple arithmetic sums and products: Are the phonological loop and the central executive involved? *Revue d'Intelligence Artificielle, 29*, 267–274.

Dehaene, S. (2014). *Le code de la conscience*. Paris: Odile Jacob.

Dehaene, S., Bossini, S., & Giraux, P. (1993). The mental representation of parity and number magnitude. *Journal of Experimental Psychology: General, 122*(3), 371–396.

Delaney, H. D. (1978). Interaction of individual differences with visual and verbal elaboration instructions. *Journal of Educational Psychology, 70*(3), 306–318.

DeSteno, D., Petty, R. E., Wegener, D. T., & Rucker, D. D. (2000). Beyond valence in the perception of likelihood: the role of emotion specificity. *Journal of Personality and Social Psychology, 78*(4), 707.

Dirkx, E., & Craik, F. I. (1992). Age related differences in memory as a function of imagery processing. *Psychology and Aging, 7*, 352–358.

Dixon, R. A. & Hultsch, D. F. (1983). Structure and development of metamemory in adulthood. *Journal of Gerontology, 38*, 682–688.

Dujardin, K., & Lemaire, P. (2008). *Neuropsychologie du vieillissement normal et pathologique*. Masson: Paris.

Dunlosky, J., & Hertzog, C. (1998). Aging and deficits in associative memory: What is the role of strategy production? *Psychology and Aging, 13*, 597–607.

Dunlosky, J., & Hertzog, C. (2001). Measuring strategy production during associative learning: The relative utility of concurrent *versus* retrospective reports. *Memory and Cognition, 29*(2), 247–253.

Duverne, S., & Lemaire, P. (2004). Age-related differences in arithmetic problem-verification strategies. *Journals of Gerontology: Series B: Psychological Sciences and Social Sciences, 59B*(3), 135–142.

Duverne, S., & Lemaire, P. (2005). Aging and arithmetic. In J. I. D. Campbell (Ed.), *The handbook of mathematical cognition* (pp. 397–412). New York: Psychology Press.

Duverne, S., Lemaire, P., & Michel, B. F. (2003). Alzheimer's disease disrupts arithmetic fact retrieval processes but not arithmetic strategy selection. *Brain and Cognition, 52*(3), 302–318.

Duverne, S., Lemaire, P., & Vandierendonck, A. (2008). Do working-memory executive components mediate the effects of age on strategy selection? Insights from arithmetic problem solving. *Psychological Research-Psychologische Forschung, 72*(1), 27–38.

El Yagoubi, R., Lemaire, P., & Besson, M. (2003). Different brain mechanisms mediate two strategies in arithmetic: evidence from event-related brain potentials. *Neuropsychologia, 41*, 855–862.

El Yagoubi, R., Lemaire, P., & Besson, M. (2005). Effects of aging on arithmetic problem-solving: An event-related brain potential study. *Journal of Cognitive Neuroscience, 17*(1), 37–50.

Elliot, A. J., Kayser, D. N., Greitemeyer, T., Lichtenfeld, S., Gramzow, R. H., Maier, M. A., & Liu, H. (2010). Red, rank, and romance in women viewing men. *Journal of Experimental Psychology: General, 139*(3), 399–417.

Eysenck, M. W. (1974). Age differences in incidental learning. *Developmental Psychology, 10*, 936–941.

Farkas, M. S., & Hoyer, W. J. (1980). Processing consequences of perceptual grouping in selective attention. *Journal of Gerontology, 35*, 207–216.

Fay, S., Isingrini, M., & Clarys, D. (2005). Effects of depth-of-processing and ageing on word-stem and word-fragment implicit memory tasks: test of the lexical-processing hypothesis. *European Journal of Cognitive Psychology, 17*, 785–802.

Fleischman, D. A., Wilson, R. S., Gabrieli, J. D. E., Bienias, J. L., & Bennett, D. A. (2004). A longitudinal study of implicit and explicit memory in old persons. *Psychology and Aging, 19*(4), 617–625.

Fodor, J. (1972). *L'explication en psychologie.* Paris: Seghers.

Folk, C. L., & Hoyer, W. J. (1992). Aging and shifts of visual spatial attention. *Psychology and Aging, 7*, 453–465.

Fradet, L., Lee, G., & Dounskaia, N. (2008). Origins of submovements in movements of elderly adults. *Journal of NeuroEngineering and Rehabilitation, 5*, 28.

Frank, D. J., Touron, D. R., & Hertzog, C. (2013). Age differences in strategy shift: Retrieval avoidance or general shift reluctance? *Psychology and Aging, 28*(3), 778–788.

Froger, C., Bouazzaoui, B., Isingrini, M., & Taconnat, L. (2012). Study-time allocation deficit of older adults: The role of environmental support at encoding. *Psychology and Aging, 27*, 577–588.

Froger, C., Taconnat, L., Landré, L., Beigneux, K., & Isingrini, M. (2009). Effects of level of processing at encoding and type of retrieval tasks in mild cognitive impairment and normal aging. *Journal of Clinical and Experimental Neuropsychology, 31*(3), 312–321.

Gandini, D., Lemaire, P., Anton, J. L., & Nazarian, B. (2008). Neural correlates of approximate quantification strategies in young and older adults: An fMRI study. *Brain Research, 1246*, 144–157.

Gandini, D., Lemaire, P., & Dufau, S. (2008). Older and younger adults' strategies in approximate quantification. *Acta Psychologica, 129*, 175–189.

Gandini, D., Lemaire, P., & Michel, B. F. (2009). Approximate quantification in young, healthy older adults, and Alzheimer patients. *Brain and Cognition, 70*, 53–61.

Geary, D., & Lin, J. (1998). Numerical cognition: Age-related differences in the speed of executing biologically primary and biologically secondary processes. *Experimental Aging Research, 24*(2), 101–138.

Geary, D. C., & Wiley, J. G. (1991). Cognitive addition: Strategy choices and speed-of-processing differences in young and elderly adults. *Psychology and Aging, 6*(3), 474–483.

Geary, D. C., Frensch, P. A., & Wiley, J. G. (1993). Simple and complex mental subtraction: Strategy choice and speed-of-processing differences in younger and older adults. *Psychology and Aging, 8*, 242–256.

Geraci, L., & Miller, T. M. (2013). Improving older adults' memory performance using prior task success. *Psychology and Aging, 28*(2), 340–345.

Geraci, L., Hughes, M. L., Miller, T. M., & De Forrest, R. (in press). The effect of prior task success on older adults' memory performance: Examining the influence of different types of task success. *Experimental Aging Research*.

Giambra, L. M., & Quilter, R. E. (1988). Sustained attention in adulthood: A unique large-sample longitudinal multicohort analysis using the Macworth Clock-Test. *Psychology and Aging, 3*, 75–83.

Graham, E. K., & Lachman, M. E. (2012). Personality stability is associated with better cognitive performance in adulthood: Are the stable more able? *Journal of Gerontology: Psychological Sciences, 67*, 545–554.

Graham, E. K., & Lachman, M. E. (2014). Personality traits, facets and cognitive performance: Age differences in their relations. *Personality and Individual Differences, 59*, 89–95.

Green, C. S., & Bavelier, D. (2008). Exercising your brain: A review of human brain plasticity and training-induced learning. *Psychology and Aging, 23*(4), 692–701.

Green, H., Lemaire, P., & Dufau, S. (2007). Eye movement correlates of younger and older adults' strategies for complex addition. *Acta Psychologica, 125*, 257–278.

Hale, S., Myerson, J., Faust, M., & Fristoe, N. (1995). Converging evidence for domain-specific slowing from multiple nonlexical tasks and multiple analytic methods. *Journal of Gerontology: Psychological Sciences, 50B*, 202–211.

Hartley, A. A. (1986). Instruction, induction, generation, and evaluation of strategies for solving search problems. *Journal of Gerontology, 41*, 650–658.

Hartley, A. A., & Anderson, J. W. (1983). Task complexity, problem representation, and problem-solving performance by younger and older adults. *Journal of Gerontology, 38*, 72–77.

Hertzog, C., & Hultsch, D.F. (2000). Metacognition in adulthood and old age. In F. I. M. Craik and T. A. Salthouse (Eds.), *The handbook of aging and cognition* (pp. 417–466). Mahwah, NJ: Erlbaum.

Hertzog, C., Lineweaver, T. T., & McGuire, C. L. (1999). Beliefs about memory and aging. In F. Blanchard-Fields & T. M. Hess (Eds.), *Social cognition and aging* (pp. 43–68). New York, NY: Academic Press.

Hertzog, C., Touron, D. R., & Hines, J. C. (2007). Does a time monitoring deficit contribute to older adults' delayed shift to retrieval during skill acquisition? *Psychology and Aging, 22*, 607–624.

Hess, T. M., Auman, C., Colcombe, S. J., & Rahhal, T. A. (2003). The impact of stereotype threat on age differences in memory performance. *The Journals of Gerontology: Series B: Psychological Sciences and Social Sciences, 58*, 3–11.

Hess, T. M., & Hinson, J. T. (2006). Age-related variation in the influences of aging stereotypes on memory in adulthood. *Psychology and Aging, 21*, 621–625.

Hess, T. M., Hinson, J. T., & Hodges, E. A. (2009). Moderators of and mechanisms underlying stereotype threat effects on older adults' memory performance. *Experimental Aging Research, 35*, 153–177.

Hess, T. M., Hinson, J. T., & Statham, J. A. (2004). Explicit and implicit stereotype activation effects on memory: Do age and awareness moderate the impact of priming? *Psychology and Aging, 19*, 495–505.

Hess, T. M., Rosenberg, D. C., & Waters, S. J. (2001). Motivation and representational processes in adulthood: The effects of social accountability and information relevance. *Psychology and Aging, 16*, 629–642.

Hinault, T., Dufau, S., & Lemaire, P. (2014). Sequential modulations of poorer-strategy effects during strategy execution: An event-related potential study in arithmetic. *Brain and Cognition, 91*(0), 123–130.

Hinault, T., Lemaire, P., & Phillips, N. (2016). Aging and sequential modulations of poorer-strategy effects: An EEG study in arithmetic problem solving. *Brain Research*, 1630, 144–158.

Hinault, T., Tiberghien, K., & Lemaire, P. (2015). Age-related differences in plausibility-checking strategies during arithmetic problem verification tasks. *The Journals of Gerontology Series B: Psychological Sciences and Social Sciences*, doi: 10.1093/geronb/gbu178.

Ho, G., & Scialfa, C. T. (2002). Age, skill transfer, and conjunction search. *Journal of Gerontology: Psychological Sciences*, 57B, 277–287.

Hodzik, S., & Lemaire, P. (2011). Inhibition and shifting capacities mediate adults' age-related differences in strategy selection and repertoire. *Acta Psychologica*, 137, 335–344.

Hommel, B., Li, K. Z. H., & Li, S. -C. (2004). Visual search across the lifespan. *Developmental Psychology*, 40, 545–558.

Jenkins, L., Myerson, J., Joerding, J. A., & Hale, S. (2000). Converging evidence that visuospatial cognition is more age-sensitive than verbal cognition. *Psychology and Aging*, 15, 157–175.

Johnson, M. M. S. (1990). Age differences in decision making: A process methodology for examining strategic information processing. *Journal of Gerontology: Psychological Sciences*, 45, 75–78.

Johnson, A., & Proctor, R. W. (2004). *Attention: Theory and practice*. Thousand Oaks, CA: Sage Publications.

Kail, M., Lemaire, P., & Lecacheur, M. (2012). Online grammaticality judgments in French young and older adults. *Experimental Aging Research*, 38, 1–22.

Ketcham, C. J., Seidler, R. D., Van Gemmert, A. W., & Stelmach, G. E. (2002). Age-related kinematic differences as influenced by task difficulty, target size, and movement amplitude. *Journals of Gerontology: Psychological Sciences and Social Sciences*, 57(1), 54–64.

Kirchhoff, B. A., Gordon, B. A., & Head, D. (2014). Prefrontal gray matter volume mediates age effects on memory strategies. *Neuroimage*, 15(90), 326–334.

Kliegel, M., & Bürki, C. (2012). Memory training interventions require a tailor-made approach. *Journal of Applied Research in Memory and Cognition*, 1, 58–60.

Kliegl, R., Smith, J., & Baltes, P. B. (1989). Testing-the-limits and the study of adult age difference in cognitive plasticity of a mnemonic skill. *Developmental Psychology*, 2, 247–256.

Kliegl, R., Smith, J., & Baltes, P. B. (1990). On the locus and process of magnification of age differences during mnemonic training. *Developmental Psychology*, 26, 894–904.

Krueger, L. E. (1986). Why 2 × 2 = 5 looks so wrong: On the odd–even rule in product verification. *Memory and Cognition*, 14(2), 141–149.

Krueger, L. E., & Hallford, E.W. (1984). Why 2 + 2 = 5 looks so wrong: On the odd–even rule in sum verification. *Memory and Cognition*, 12, 171–180.

Kuhlmann, B. G., & Touron, D. R. (2012). Mediator-based encoding strategies in source monitoring in young and older adults. *Journal of Experimental Psychology: Learning, Memory, and Cognition*, 38(5), 1352–1364.

Lachman, M. E., & Tun, P. A. (2008). Cognitive testing in large-scale surveys: Assessment by telephone. In S. Hofer & D. Alwin (Eds.), *Handbook on cognitive aging: Interdisciplinary perspectives* (pp. 506–522). Thousand Oaks, CA: Sage Publishers.

Lemaire, P. (2010). Cognitive strategy variations during aging. *Current Direction in Psychological Science*, 19(6), 363–369.

Lemaire, P., & Arnaud, L. (2008). Young and older adults' strategies in complex arithmetic. *American Journal of Psychology*, 121(1), 1–16.

Lemaire, P., Arnaud, L., & Lecacheur, M. (2004). Adults' age-related differences in adaptivity of strategy choices: Evidence from computational estimation. *Psychology and Aging*, 10(3), 467–481.

Lemaire, P., & Bherer, L. (2005). *Psychologie du vieillissement. Une perspective cognitive*. Brussels: De Boeck.

Lemaire, P., & Fayol, M. (1995). When plausibility judgments supersede fact retrieval: The example of the odd–even effect on product verification. *Memory and Cognition, 23*(1), 34–48.

Lemaire, P., & Hinault, T. (2014). Age-related differences in sequential modulations of poorer-strategy effects: A study in arithmetic problem solving. *Experimental Psychology, 61*(4), 253–262.

Lemaire, P., & Lecacheur, M. (2001). Older and younger adults' strategy use and execution in currency conversion tasks: Insights from French franc to euro and euro to French franc conversions. *Journal of Experimental Psychology: Applied, 3*, 195–206.

Lemaire, P., & Lecacheur, M. (2007). Aging and numerosity estimation. *Journal of Gerontology: Psychological Sciences, 62*, 305–312.

Lemaire, P., & Lecacheur, M. (2010). Strategy switch costs in arithmetic problem solving. *Memory and Cognition, 38*(3), 322–332.

Lemaire, P., & Leclère, M. (2014a). Strategy repetition in young and older adults: A study in arithmetic. *Developmental Psychology, 50*(2), 460–468.

Lemaire, P., & Leclère, M. (2014b). Strategy selection in Alzheimer patients: A study in arithmetic. *Journal of Experimental and Clinical Neuropsychology, 36*(5), 507–516.

Lemaire, P., & Reder, L. (1999). What affects strategy selection in arithmetic? An example of parity and five effects on product verification. *Memory and Cognition, 22*, 364–382.

Lemaire, P., & Siegler, R. S. (1995). Four aspects of strategic change: Contributions to children's learning of multiplication. *Journal of Experimental Psychology: General, 124*(1), 83–97.

Lemaire, P., Lecacheur, M., & Ferréol-Barbey, M. (2001). Strategy choices in conversion tasks: The examples of French franc to euro and euro to French franc conversions. *Current Psychology Letters, 4*, 39–50.

Levy, B. (1996). Improving memory in old age through implicit self-stereotyping. *Journal of Personality and Social Psychology, 71*, 1092–1107.

Li, S.-C., Schmiedek, F., Huxhold, O., Röcke, C., Smith, J., & Lindenberger, U. (2008). Working memory plasticity in old age: Practice gain, transfer, and maintenance. *Psychology and Aging, 23*, 731–742.

Li, Y., Baldassi, M., Johnson, E. J., & Weber, E. U. (2013). Complementary cognitive capabilities, economic decision making, and aging. *Psychology and Aging, 28*(3), 595–613.

Light, L. L., & Zelinski, E. M. (1983). Memory for spatial information in young and old adults. *Developmental Psychology, 19*, 901–906.

Lima, S. D., Hale, S., & Myerson, J. (1991). How general is general slowing? Evidence from the lexical domain. *Psychology and Aging, 7*, 585–593.

Loewen, E. R., Shaw, R. J., & Craik, F. I. M. (1990). Age differences in components of metamemory. *Experimental Aging Research, 16*, 43–48.

Lövdén, M., Schmiedek, F., Kennedy, K. M., Rodrigue, K. M., Lindenberger, U., & Raz, N. (2013). Does variability in cognitive performance correlate with frontal brain volume? *Neuroimage, 1*(64), 209–215.

Lustig, C., & Flegal, K. E. (2008). Targeting latent function: Encouraging effective encoding for successful memory training and transfer. *Psychology and Aging, 23*, 754–764.

Luwel, K., Onghena, P., Torbeyns, J., Schillemans, V., & Verschaffel, L. (2009). Strengths and weaknesses of the choice/no-choice method in research on strategy use. *European Psychologist, 14* (4), 351–362.

Lyketsos, C. G., Chen, L. S., & Anthony, J. C. (1999). Cognitive decline in adulthood: An 11.5 years follow-up of the Baltimore Epidemiological Catchment Area study. *American Journal of Psychiatry, 156*, 58–65.

Madden, D. J. (1988). Adult age differences in the effects of sentence context and stimulus degradation during visual word recognition. *Psychology and Aging, 3*(2), 167–172.

Maquestiaux, F. (2013). *Psychologie de l'attention*. Brussels: De Boeck University.

Maquestiaux, F., Didierjean, A., Ruthruff, E., Chauvel, G., & Hartley, A. A. (2013). Lost ability to automatize task performance in old age. *Psychonomic Bulletin and Review, 20*, 1206–1212.

Masse, C., & Lemaire, P. (2001). How do people choose among strategies? A case study of parity and five-rule effects in arithmetical problem solving. *Psychological Research, 65*(1), 28–33.

Masse, C., Lecacheur, M., & Lemaire, P. (2000). Strategy choice in French francs/euros conversion task. *International Journal of Psychology, 35*, 3–4.

Mata, R., & Nunes, L. (2010). When less is enough: Cognitive aging, information search, and decision quality in consumer choice. *Psychology and Aging, 25*, 289–298.

Mata, R., Schooler, L. J., & Rieskamp, J. (2007). The aging decision maker: Cognitive aging and the adaptive selection of decision strategies. *Psychology and Aging, 22*(4), 796–810.

Mata, R., Wilke, A., & Czienskowski, U. (2009). Cognitive aging and adaptive foraging behavior. *Journal of Gerontology: Psychological Sciences, 64B*(4), 474–481.

Mather, M., & Carstensen, L. L. (2003). Aging and attentional biases for emotional faces. *Psychological Science, 14*, 409–415.

Mather, M., & Carstensen, L. L. (2005). Aging and motivated cognition: The positivity effect in attention and memory. *Trends in Cognitive Sciences, 9*, 496–502.

Mathy, P., & Van der Linden, M. (1995). Effet de l'âge et du niveau scolaire sur la sensibilité à l'interférence proactive dans la mémorisation de récits. *Bulletin de Psychologie, 48*, 498–501.

Matthews, G. (2009). Personality and performance: Cognitive processes and models. In P. J. Corr & G. Matthews (Eds.), *The Cambridge handbook of personality psychology*. Cambridge: Cambridge University Press.

McArdle, J. J., & Prindle, J. J. (2008). A latent change score analysis of a randomized clinical trial in reasoning training. *Psychology and Aging, 23*(4), 702–719.

McCalley, L. T., Bouwhuis, D. G., & Juola, J. F. (1995). Age changes in the distribution of visual attention. *Journal of Gerontology, 50B*(6), 316–331.

McCrae, R. (1987). Creativity, divergent thinking, and openness to experience. *Journal of Personality and Social Psychology, 52*(6), 1258–1265.

Meiran, N. (2010). Task switching: Mechanisms underlying rigid vs. flexible self control. In R. Hassin, K. Ochsner, & Y. Trope (Eds.), *Social cognition and social neuroscience* (pp. 202–221). New York, NY: Oxford University Press.

Mikels, J. A., Larkin, G. R., Reuter-Lorenz, P. A., & Carstensen, L. L. (2005). Divergent trajectories in the aging mind: Changes in working memory for affective versus visual information with age. *Psychology and Aging, 20*(4), 542–553.

Mitchell, D. B. (1989). How many memory systems? Evidence from aging. *Journal of Experimental Psychology: Learning, Memory and Cognition, 15*, 31–49.

Moberg, P., & Raz, N. (1997). Aging and olfactory recognition memory: Effect of encoding strategies and cognitive abilities. *The International Journal of Neuroscience, 90*(3–4), 277–291.

Moore, S. C., & Oaksford, M. (2002). Some long-term effects of emotion on cognition. *British Journal of Psychology, 93*, 383–395.

Moutafi, J., Furnham, A., & Paltiel, L. (2005). Can personality factors predict intelligence? *Personality and Individual Differences, 38*, 1021–1033.

Moyer, R. S., & Landauer, T. K. (1967). The time required for judgments of numerical inequality. *Nature, 215*, 1519–1520.

Naveh-Benjamin, M., Brav, T. K., & Levy, O. (2007). The associative memory deficit of older adults: The role of strategy utilization. *Psychology and Aging, 22*(1), 202–208.

Naveh-Benjamin, M., Craik, F. I. M., Guez, J., & Kreuger, S. (2005). Divided attention in younger and older adults: Effects of strategy and relatedness on memory performance and secondary task costs. *Journal of Experimental Psychology: Learning, Memory and Cognition, 32*, 520–537.

Newell, A., & Simon, H. A. (1972). *Human problem solving.* Englewood Cliffs, NJ: Prentice-Hall.

Nicolas, S., Ehrlich, M. F., & Facci, G. (1996). Implicit memory and aging: Generation effect in a word-stem completion test. *Cahiers de Psychologie Cognitive, 15*(5), 513–533.

Niedenthal, P. M., & Setterlund, M. B. (1994). Emotion congruence in perception. *Personality and Social Psychology Bulletin, 20*(4), 401–411.

Nyberg, L., Sandblom, J., Jones, S., Stigsdotter Neely, A., Petersson, K. M., Ingvar, M., & Bäckman, L. (2003). Neural correlates of training-related memory improvement in adulthood and aging. *Proceedings of the National Academy of Sciences, USA, 100*, 13728–13733.

Onyper, S. V., Hoyer, W. J., & Cerella, J. (2006). Determinants of retrieval solutions during cognitive skill training: Source confusions. *Memory and Cognition, 34*, 538–549.

Onyper, S. V., Hoyer, W. J., & Cerella, J. (2008). Effects of item difficulty on the retrieval of solutions during cognitive skill acquisition: Age differences. *Aging, Neuropsychology, and Cognition, 15*, 358–383.

Osorio, A., Ballesteros, S., Fay, S., & Pouthas, V. (2009). The effect of age on word-stem cued recall: A behavioral and electrophysiological study. *Brain Research, 1289*, 56–68.

Osorio, A., Fay, S., Pouthas, V., & Ballesteros, S. (2010). Ageing affects brain activity in highly educated older adults: An ERP study using a word-stem priming task. *Cortex, 46*, 522–534.

Overton, W. F. (1990). Competence and procedures: Constraints on the development of logical reasoning. In W. F. Overton (Ed.), *Reasoning, necessity and logic: Developmental perspectives* (pp. 1–32). Hillsdale, N J: Erlbaum.

Park, D. C., & Bischof, G. N. (2013). The aging mind: Neuroplasticity in response to cognitive training. *Dialogues in Clinical Neuroscience, 15*, 109–119.

Park, D. C., & Shaw, R. J. (1992). Effect of environmental support on implicit and explicit memory in younger and older adults. *Psychology and Aging, 7*(4), 632–642.

Park, D. C., Lodi-Smith, J., Drew, L. M., Haber, S. H., Hebrank, A. C., Bischof, G. N., & Aamodt, W. (2013). The impact of sustained engagement on cognitive function in older adults: The Synapse Project. *Psychological Science, 15*(1), 109–119.

Pashler, H. (1998). *The psychology of attention.* Cambridge, MA: MIT Press.

Paterson, K. B., McGowan, V. A., & Jordan, T. R. (2013). Filtered text reveals adult age differences in reading. *Psychology and Aging, 28*, 352–364.

Pena-Casanova, J., Sanchez-Benavides, G., de Sola, S., Manero-Borras, R. M., & Casals-Coll, M. (2012). Neuropsychology of Alzheimer's disease. *Archives of Medical Research, 43*, 686–693.

Pessoa, L. (2012). Beyond brain regions: Network perspective of cognition–emotion interactions. *Behavioral and Brain Sciences, 35*, 158–159.

Piolino, P., Desgranges, B., Belliard, S., Matuszewski, V., Lalevée, C., de La Sayette, V., & Eustache, F. (2003). Autobiographical memory and autonoetic consciousness: Triple dissociation in neurodegenerative diseases. *Brain, 126*, 2203–2219.

Poletti, C., Sleimen-Malkoun, R., Temprado, J. J., & Lemaire, P. (2015). Older and younger adults' strategies in sensori-motor tasks: Insights from Fitts' pointing task. *Journal of Experimental Psychology: Human Perception and Performance,* (in press).

Queen, T. L., & Hess, T. M. (2010). Age differences in the effects of conscious and unconscious thought in decision making. *Psychology and Aging, 25,* 251–261.

Rahhal, T. A., Hasher, L., & Colcombe, S. J. (2001). Instructional manipulations and age differences in memory: Now you see them, now you don't. *Psychology and Aging, 16,* 697–706.

Rahhal, T. A., May, C. P., & Hasher, L. (2002). Truth and character: Sources that older adults can remember. *Psychological Science, 13,* 101–105.

Ravdin, L. D., & Katzen, H. L. (Eds.) (2013). *Handbook on the neuropsychology of aging and dementia.* New York: Springer Science.

Raz, N. (2000). Aging of the brain and its impact on cognitive performance: Integration of structural and functional findings. In F. I. M. Craik & T. A. Salthouse (Eds.), *The handbook of aging and cognition.* Mahwah, NJ: Lawrence Erlbaum.

Reder, L., Wible, C., & Martin, J. (1986). Differential memory changes with age: Exact retrieval versus plausible inference. *Journal of Experimental Psychology: Learning, Memory, and Cognition, 12,* 72–81.

Reichle, E. D., Carpenter, P. A., & Just, M. A. (2000). The neural bases of strategy and skill in sentence-picture verification. *Cognitive Psychology, 40,* 261–295.

Roberts, B. W., & DelVecchio, W. F. (2000). The rank-order consistency of personality traits from childhood to old age: A quantitative review of longitudinal studies. *Psychological Bulletin, 126,* 3–25.

Rogers, W. A., Hertzog, C., & Fisk, A. D. (2000). An individual differences analysis of ability and strategy influences: Age-related differences in associative learning. *Journal of Experimental Psychology: Learning, Memory, and Cognition, 26*(2), 359–394.

Rozencwajg, P., Cherfi, M., Ferrandez, A. M., Lautrey, J., Lemoine, C., & Loarer, E. (2005). Age related changes in the strategies used by middle aged adults to solve a block design task. *The International Journal of Aging and Human Development, 60*(2), 159–182.

Rypma, B., Berger J. S., Genova, H. M., Rebbechi, D., & D'Esposito, M. (2005). Dissociating age-related changes in cognitive strategy and neural efficiency using event-related fMRI. *Cortex, 41,* 582–594.

Salthouse, T. A. (1984). Effects of age and skill in typing. *Journal of Experimental Psychology: General, 113*(3), 357–362.

Salthouse, T. A. (1992). Why do adult age differences increase with task complexity? *Developmental Psychology, 28*(5), 905–918.

Salthouse, T. A. (1996). The processing-speed theory of adult age differences in cognition. *Psychological Review, 103,* 403–428.

Salthouse, T. A. (2009a). When does age-related cognitive decline begin? *Neurobiology of Aging, 30,* 507–514.

Salthouse, T. A. (2009b). Decomposing age correlations on neuropsychological and cognitive variables. *Journal of the International Neuropsychological Society, 15,* 650–661.

Salthouse, T. A. (2010a). Influence of age on practice effects in longitudinal neurocognitive change. *Neuropsychology, 24* (5), 563–572.

Salthouse, T. A. (2010b). *Major issues in cognitive aging.* New York: Oxford University Press.

Salthouse, T. A. (2014). Selectivity of attrition in longitudinal studies of cognitive functioning. *Journal of Gerontology: Psychological Sciences, 69,* 567–574.

Salthouse, T. A., & Prill, K. A. (1987). Inferences about age impairments in inferential reasoning. *Psychology and Aging, 2,* 43–51.

Schaie, K. W. (1996). *Intellectual development in adulthood.* Cambridge: Cambridge University Press.

Schaie, K. W. (2005). *Developmental influences on adult intelligence: The Seattle longitudinal study.* New York: Oxford University Press.

Schaie, K. W., & Willis, S. L. (1986). Can decline in adult intellectual functioning be reversed? *Developmental Psychology, 22*, 222–232.

Schaie, K. W., Willis, S. L., & Caskie, G. I. L. (2004). The Seattle longitudinal study: Relation between personality and cognition. *Aging, Neuropsychology and Cognition, 11*, 204–234.

Shake, M. C., Noh, S. R., & Stine-Morrow, E. L. (2009). Age differences in learning from text: Evidence for functionally distinct text processing systems. *Applied Cognitive Psychology, 23*(4), 561–578.

Siegler, R. S., & Lemaire, P. (1997). Older and younger adults' strategy choices in multiplication: Testing predictions of ASCM using the choice/no-choice method. *Journal of Experimental Psychology: General, 126*(1), 71–92.

Siegler, R. S., Stern, E. (1998). Conscious and unconscious strategy discoveries: A microgenetic analysis. *Journal of Experimental Psychology: General, 127*, 377–397.

Sitzer, D. I., Twamley, E. W., & Jeste, D. V. (2006). Cognitive training in Alzheimer's disease: A meta-analysis of the literature. Acta *Psychiatrica Scandinavica, 114*, 85–90.

Sliwinski, M. (1997). Aging and counting speed: Evidence for process-specific slowing. *Psychology and Aging, 12*, 38–49.

Small, B. J., Hultsch, D.F., & Masson, M.E.J. (1995). Adult age differences in perceptually-based, but not conceptually-based implicit tests of memory. *Journal of Gerontology: Psychological Sciences, 50B*, 162–170.

Smith, A. D. (1977). Adult age differences in cued recall. *Developmental Psychology, 13*, 326–331.

Soubelet, A. (2011). Age–cognition relations and the personality trait of conscientiousness. *Journal of Research in Personality, 45*(6), 529–534.

Soubelet, A., & Salthouse, T. A. (2011). Personality–cognition relations across adulthood. *Developmental Psychology, 47*(2), 303–310.

Stein, R., Blanchard-Fields, F., & Hertzog, C. (2002). The effects of age stereotype priming on the memory performance of older adults. *Experimental Aging Research, 28*, 169–181.

Stine, E. L. (1990). On-line processing of written text by younger and older adults. *Psychology and Aging, 5*, 68–78.

Stine-Morrow, E. A. L., Loveless, M. K., & Soederberg, L. K. (1996). Resource allocation in on-line reading by younger and older adults. *Psychology and Aging, 11*(3), 475–486.

Stine-Morrow, E. A. L., Miller, L. M. S., & Hertzog, C. (2006). Aging and self-regulated language processing. *Psychological Bulletin, 132*, 582–606.

Stine-Morrow, E. A. L., Shake, M. C., Miles, J. R., Lee, K., & McConkie, G. (2010). Pay now or pay later: Aging and the role of boundary salience in self-regulation of conceptual integration in sentence processing. *Psychology and Aging, 25*, 168–176.

Strough, J., McFall, J. P., Flinn, J. A., & Schuller, K. L. (2008). Collaborative everyday problem solving among same-gender friends in early and later adulthood. *Psychology and Aging, 23*, 517–530.

Taconnat, L., Clarys, D., Vanneste, S., Bouazzaoui, B., & Isingrini, M. (2007). Aging and strategic retrieval in a cued-recall test: The role of executive functions and fluid intelligence. *Brain and Cognition, 64*, 1–6.

Taconnat, L., & Isingrini, M. (2004). Cognitive operations in the generation effect on a recall test: Role of aging and divided attention. *Journal of Experiment Psychology: Learning, Memory, and Cognition, 30*(4), 827–837.

Takahashi, M., & Overton, W. (1996). Formal reasoning in Japanese older adults: The role of metacognition strategy, task content, and social factors. *Journal of Adult Development, 3*(2), 81–91.

Tournier, I., & Postal, V. (2011). Strategy selection and aging: Impact of item concreteness in paired-associated task. *Aging, Neuropsychology and Cognition, 18*(2), 195–213.

Touron, D. R. (2006). Are item-level strategy shifts abrupt and collective? Age differences in cognitive skill acquisition. *Psychonomic Bulletin and Review, 13*, 781–786.

Touron, D. R., & Hertzog, C. (2004). Distinguishing age differences in knowledge, strategy use, and confidence during strategic skill acquisition. *Psychology and Aging, 19*, 452–466.

Touron, D. R., & Hertzog, C. (2009). Age differences in strategic behavior during a computation-based skill acquisition task. *Psychology and Aging, 24*, 574–585.

Trick, L. M., Enns, J. T., & Brodeur, D. A. (1996). Life-span changes in visual enumeration: The number discrimination task. *Developmental Psychology, 32*, 925–932.

Uittenhove, K., Burger, L., Taconnat, L., & Lemaire, P. (2015). Sequential difficulty effects during execution of memory strategies in young and older adults. *Memory, 23*(6), 806–816.

Uittenhove, K., & Lemaire, P. (2012). Sequential difficulty effects during strategy execution: A study in arithmetic. *Experimental Psychology, 59*(5), 295–301.

Uittenhove, K., & Lemaire, P. (2013a). Strategy sequential difficulty effects vary with working-memory and response-stimulus intervals: A study in arithmetic. *Acta Psychologica, 143*, 113–118.

Uittenhove, K., & Lemaire, P. (2013b). Strategy sequential difficulty effects in Alzheimer patients: A study in arithmetic. *Journal of Clinical and Experimental Neuropsychology, 35*(1), 83–89.

Uittenhove, K., Poletti, C., Dufau, S., & Lemaire, P. (2013). The time course of strategy sequential difficulty effects: An ERP study in arithmetic. *Experimental Brain Research, 227*, 1–8.

Vandierendonck, A., Liefooghe, B., & Verbruggen, F. (2010). Task switching: Interplay of reconfiguration and interference control. *Psychological Bulletin, 136*(4), 601–626.

Vecchi, T., & Cornoldi, C. (1999). Passive storage and active manipulation in visuo-spatial working memory: Further evidence from the study of age differences. *European Journal of Cognitive Psychology, 11*, 391–406.

Veiel, L. L., Storandt, M., & Abrams, R. A. (2006). Visual search for change. *Psychology and Aging, 21*, 754–762.

Vieillard, S., & Bigand, E. (2014). Distinct effects of positive and negative music on older adults' auditory target identification performances. *The Quarterly Journal of Experimental Psychology, 67*(11), 2225–2238.

Vieillard, S., Didierjean, A., & Maquestiaux, F. (2012). Changes in the perception and the psychological structure of musical emotions with advancing age. *Experimental Aging Research, 38*(4), 422–441.

Von Helversen, B., & Mata, R. (2012). Losing a dime with a satisfied mind: Positive affect predicts less search in sequential decision making. *Psychology and Aging, 77*(4), 825–839.

Wason, P. C. (1983). Realism and rationality in the selection task. In J. St. B. T. Evans (Ed.), *Thinking and reasoning: Psychological approaches*. London: Routledge & Kegan Paul.

Watson, D. G., Maylor, E. A., & Bruce, L. A. M. (2005). Search, enumeration, and aging: Eye movement requirements cause age-equivalent performance in enumeration but not in search tasks. *Psychology and Aging, 20*(2), 226–240.

Watson, D. G., Maylor, E. A., & Manson, N. J. (2002). Aging and enumeration: A selective deficit for the subitization of targets among distractors. *Psychology and Aging and Mental Health, 17*, 496–504.

Willis, S., & Boron, J. (2008). Midlife cognition: The association of personality with cognition and risk of cognitive impairment. In S. Hofer & D. Alwin (Eds.), *Handbook of cognitive aging: Interdisciplinary perspectives.* (pp. 647–661). Thousand Oaks, CA: SAGE Publications.

Winocur, G., Moscovitch, M., & Stuss, D.T. (1996). Explicit and implicit memory in the elderly: Evidence for double dissociation involving medial temporal- and frontal-lobe functions. *Neuropsychology, 10,* 57–65.

Wisleder, D., & Dounskaia, N. (2007). The role of different submovement types during pointing to a target. *Experimental Brain Research, 176*(1), 132–149.

Worthy, D. A., & Maddox, W. T. (2012). Age-based differences in strategy-use in choice tasks. *Frontiers in Neuroscience, 5*(145), 1–10.

Wotschack, C., & Kliegl, R. (2013). Reading strategy modulates parafoveal-on-foveal effects in sentence reading. *Quarterly Journal of Experimental Psychology, 66*(3), 548–562.

Yiend, J. (2010). The effects of emotion on attention: A review of attentional processing of emotional information. *Cognition and Emotion, 24*(1), 3–47.

Yonelinas, A. P. (2002). The nature of recollection and familiarity: A review of 30 years of research. *Journal of Memory and Language, 46,* 441–517.

Zbrodoff, N. J., & Logan, G. D. (2005). What everyone finds: The problem size effect. In J. I. D. Campbell (Ed.), *Handbook of mathematical cognition* (pp. 331–345). New York: Psychology Press.

Zeelenberg, M., & Pieters, R. (2007). A theory of regret regulation 1.0. *Journal of Consumer Psychology, 17,* 3–18.

Zinke, K., Zeintl, M., Rose, N. S., Putzmann, J., Pydde, A., & Kliegel, M. (2014). Working memory training and transfer in older adults: Effects of age, baseline performance, and training gains. *Developmental Psychology, 50,* 304–315.

AUTHOR INDEX

SUBJECT INDEX